WHAT WAS THE OXFORD MOVEMENT?

WHAT WAS THE OXFORD MOVEMENT?

George Herring

continuum
LONDON • NEW YORK

Continuum

The Tower Building, 11 York Road, London SE1 7NX
370 Lexington Avenue, New York, NY 10017–6503
www.continuumbooks.com

© George Herring 2002

British Library Cataloguing-in-Publication Data

A catalogue record for this book is available from the British Library.

ISBN 0–8264–5186-1

Typeset by YHT Ltd, London
Printed and bound by Biddles Ltd, Guildford and King's Lynn

For my mother, and in memory of my father

Contents

Preface

'What was the Oxford Movement?' is a question I have been asked on numerous occasions by friends, family, colleagues and especially students. And when they have followed that with the further question 'What shall I read?', this has presented me with a problem since there is no single volume that attempts to answer the question that I could point to without qualification. Most of the older narrative histories are now very dated in terms of content, interpretation and style, while modern scholarship on the Movement has tended to concentrate on specialist monographs concerned mainly with very specific aspects. There is no one book that I could recommend as a good up-to-date starting point to introduce the enquiring student to the history of Tractarianism. This was further reinforced when in 1994 I was invited by the Vicar of Wantage, Revd John Salter, to give a lecture to his parishioners about their nineteenth-century Tractarian vicar, William Butler; enthusiastic lay people who wanted to find out more about the tradition Butler represented were faced with the same difficulties as my students. The genesis of this book originated in a shared frustration on the part of both the teacher and the learner.

This book is therefore an attempt to answer a question, and to provide that up-to-date starting point for investigating the Oxford Movement. It is not a narrative history but rather adopts an approach which, for want of a better term, I would call cumulative, progressively building an understanding of Tractarianism in stages. In so doing it not only attempts to synthesize some of the best modern research on the Movement, but also to break new ground in a number of areas, not least in re-evaluating the effect on the Movement of Newman's conversion to Roman Catholicism in 1845, and in providing a long-overdue account of the impact of

Tractarianism within the parochial setting, including a large amount of new statistical and geographical data. At a number of points there is a critical re-examination of some of the myths that have grown up about the Oxford Movement, which may surprise readers who are only familiar with the older literature. In addition, I have provided a selection of 40 documents, varying considerably in length, ranging from novels to sermons to poetry, extracts from both the Tractarians themselves and their critics, many of which have never been reproduced since they were first written. These are designed to be both an integral part of the main text, and to stand on their own as a separated collection. Finally, I have added an Epilogue which offers some thoughts on the contemporary problems faced by Anglo-Catholics, including the controversy over the ordination of women, in the light of the historical experience of Tractarianism.

I first encountered the Oxford Movement in an academic sense at Leicester University when I read Newman's *Apologia*, one of the set texts for my Special Subject, Victorian England. This was followed by my MA dissertation on Dr Pusey at the Victorian Studies Centre in Leicester. My enthusiasm now fired, I proceeded to Keble College, Oxford, to research for a doctorate in post-1845 Tractarianism under the supervision of the then Fellow and Chaplain, Revd Dr Geoffrey Rowell. Out of all the debts of gratitude I have accumulated over the years leading up to the writing of this book, the ones to Bishop Geoffrey, as he now is, stand out, not only for his immense learning, but also for his constant readiness to share his fund of wisdom with others. Without him this book would never have been written. Among the many others with whom I have discussed the Oxford Movement over the years I would particularly wish to mention Dr Peter Nockles, Dr Peter Toon, Revd Dr Kenneth Noakes, and the latter's successor as Librarian at Pusey House, Revd Peter Cobb. More recently my colleague and friend, Dr Robert Whiting, has imparted some interesting insights from the perspective of his own researches on the English Reformation. And my wife, Catherine, herself a history graduate, has been the best 'critical friend' I could have wished for; her persistence and belief kept me going forward in the writing of this book even during the darkest moments of its production. However, I am entirely responsible for the authorial interpretations and opinions, and am conscious of the book's limitations especially in terms of what I have not covered. But in order to contain it within a reasonable length, selectivity was essential.

I would also like to thank Dr Peter Durrant and his staff at the Berkshire County Record Office for all the help they gave me when I was reading the invaluable, if voluminous, manuscript pages of the *Wantage Parish Diaries* of William Butler, and Thomas Stevens's *Letter Books*. The staff of the Bodleian Library in Oxford delivered several hundred nineteenth-century volumes to me without a single mistake. And the staff of the Minster Library in York supplied me with a number of crucial texts during the actual writing of the book. Once again my thanks go to Catherine for typing the text. And finally an especial thank you to my children, Eleanor and Edward, for their support and patience during the writing and typing of this book, and for having two historians for parents.

Introduction

Interpretations past and present

Since the Reformation there have been only a handful of movements of what might be termed revitalization that could be said to have left a permanent mark on the face of Christianity in the English-speaking world. Puritanism in the late sixteenth and early seventeenth centuries, and the Evangelical reawakening that began in the middle of the eighteenth century clearly belong to this select group. And then there is the Oxford Movement. So pronounced was its influence in Victorian England that today it is 'virtually impossible to read an account' of religion in that period without coming across it.[1] At its most extreme modern readers might even be led to believe that 'the only significant group' in the Church of England in those years consisted of its followers.[2] Yet at first glance this seems rather strange, for its duration appears to have been relatively short and its adherents few in number. In addition, while in many ways it shared common features with earlier movements, it was at the same time radically different in its rejection of the Protestant Reformation and glorification of the Catholic past.

If the modern reader finds this perplexing, then he or she is only reflecting the initial reaction of many people when the Movement first appeared in the 1830s. The early literary products from these Fellows of Oxford Colleges were difficult to categorize, as they seemed to fit no conventional ecclesiastical party label; here was something genuinely new. But as time passed and their aims and views were elaborated, perplexity began to give way to a polarization between those who were coming more and more to admire these writers, and those who increasingly feared and loathed them.

1

For some they were champions of Church liberty, for others traitors to the Protestant inheritance.

Almost inevitably these radically opposed views not only became entrenched among Victorian churchmen, but were also reflected in the early historical accounts of the Movement. One tradition emerged which tended to portray the originators of the Movement in heroic terms, a small but courageous band of reformers battling against the forces of a hostile Establishment, an enraged Protestantism, and a growing liberal tendency in theology. This school perhaps reached its apogee in 1915 when S. L. Ollard published his *Short History of the Oxford Movement,* the opening paragraph of which sets the scene for what was an unashamedly celebratory chronicle [Document 1]. The alternative tradition saw the Movement in very different terms. For these writers the Oxford men were not heroes but rather villains secretly believing the doctrines of Rome and attempting to subvert the true Protestant faith of Englishmen. This type of account attained its most substantial form in the works of Walter Walsh published at the end of the nineteenth century, the very titles of whose books proclaimed his views: *The Secret History of the Oxford Movement,* and *The History of the Romeward Movement in the Church of England 1833–1864* [Document 2].

However, with the publication of *The Anglican Revival: Studies in the Oxford Movement* in 1925 by the Swedish scholar, Yngve Brilioth, the overtly partisan tone of the earlier works began to diminish. But at the same time as a more ecumenical approach to Oxford Movement studies emerged, too many later authors still relied very heavily on the writings of a relative handful of the originators of the Movement: John Henry Newman, John Keble, Edward Bouverie Pusey, Richard Hurrell Froude and a few others still provide the main sources of material for modern scholarship. A notable attempt to switch the focus from this 'inner core' came in 1966 when David Newsome wrote *The Parting of Friends: A Study of the Wilberforces and Henry Manning* but even this only shifted the spotlight from one small group to another equally restricted collection of individuals. All great *movements,* whether in the religious or other spheres of activity, by their very nature not only have originators, but also supporters and successors. The Oxford Movement is no exception, but often those who write about it still seem to rely too much on a 'great men' view of history. In recent decades the study of other movements has tended to break away from this concentration on individuals. The Enlightenment is a case in point. Traditionally, accounts of this intellectual movement had dwelt at length on the works of Voltaire, Rousseau and a few others; in the last generation, however, historians have come to see that this approach can distort more than clarify a phenomenon that was widespread across Europe and involved a multitude of writers and sympathizers.[3] While clearly not as extensive in its influence, by the time that Newman left the Church of his birth for the Roman Communion in 1845, the Oxford Movement had grown far beyond the confines of the university, and its sympathizers were diffused across the parishes of England. One of the purposes of this present study is to expand our understanding of the Oxford Movement. Of course its originators in the 1830s were crucial in setting into motion ideas and theories about Anglicanism, but it was largely others who put them into practice. As Newman himself argued in the early days of the Movement, in the very first of the *Tracts for the Times,* the ideas he was advancing represented 'a serious practical question' and not just an abstruse theory.[4] However, it was mainly a small army of largely unknown parochial clergy who laboured to realize the vision of Anglicanism that Newman and his friends first conceived in Oxford. Without them that vision would not have become a *movement* in a practical sense. Part of this study will, therefore, be devoted to examining how they put into practice in their parishes the theories first enunciated in the university, and thus will widen the focus of the Movement somewhat from a concentration on its first leaders, to include its subsequent clerical sympathizers.

While the number of adherents the Oxford Movement drew into its orbit was greater than might at first be imagined from reading some of the historical literature, at the same time its duration was also more extensive. That will lead us into a consideration of dates: when did it begin, and when did it end? The traditional starting point of the Movement was 14 July 1833, when Keble preached his Assize Sermon on the subject of National Apostasy from the pulpit of the University Church in Oxford. Newman gave his own *imprimatur* to this date in 1864 when he wrote in his *Apologia*: 'I have ever considered and kept the day, as the start of the religious movement of 1833.'[5] That date, along with the publication of the first of the *Tracts for the Times* on 9 September 1833, has entered firmly into the mythology of the Movement, and many modern histories of the nineteenth-century Church continue to quote 1833 as the starting point of the Movement.[6] However, recent specialist studies tend to be far less certain about the importance of the events of 1833, and some tend to push the starting date back into the 1820s. That raises the whole question of whether or not it is now possible to give a definitive answer to when the Movement started and, indeed, whether it matters.

On the other hand, many traditional narrative accounts of the Oxford Movement end in 1845. The crucial moment here is the morning of 9 October when the Passionist priest, Father Dominic Barberi, formally received John Henry Newman into the Roman Catholic Church, and the man who had come to be acknowledged as the leader of the Movement left it, believing it to have proved itself flawed. In 1891 R. W. Church's history was published: *The Oxford Movement: Twelve Years 1833–1845* subsequently came to be recognized as the 'classic' account, and as late as 1969 Marvin O'Connell's substantial narrative still followed this same formula, ending with Newman's conversion.[7] However, neither Church nor O'Connell actually believed that the Movement ended in 1845, even if their accounts did. The problem is that continuing a narrative after 1845 becomes extraordinarily difficult: as Church wrote: 'All the world knows that it was not, in fact, killed or even arrested by the shock of 1845. But after 1845, its field was at least as much out of Oxford as in it.'[8] By that date the Movement had expanded so much both in terms of personalities and geographical extent that a narrative approach to its history is virtually impossible. Unfortunately, so intense has been the scrutiny of those twelve years and the handful of individuals at the heart of them, that relatively little is known about the Movement in subsequent decades. This book aims to remedy that to some extent, not by a narrative method, but rather by exploring some of the themes of parochial Tractarianism, especially in the twenty years or so after 1845.

Another problem the modern reader encounters when studying the Oxford Movement is the sheer wealth of material. In the last half-century the fashion for approaching it through narrative has tended to give way to a series of often quite substantial specialist monographs on particular aspects of the Movement. For those students not already familiar with the basic history, ideas and personalities of the Movement, this can prove to be rather daunting, not least in terms of the time required to read them. Some of these works have been invaluable in illuminating or reinterpreting crucial areas, such as Alf Härdelin's 1965 study *The Tractarian Understanding of the Eucharist*, Peter Toon's work on the Evangelical response to the Oxford Movement published in 1979, Rune Imberg's detailed study of 1987 of the published *Tracts* through all

4

their various nineteenth-century editions, the 1991 work by Stephen Thomas, *Newman and Heresy*, a scholarly investigation of Newman's response to the early Church, Peter Nockles' work on the relationship between the Oxford Movement and the older High Churchmen, *The Oxford Movement in Context*, published in 1994, and a study of Ritualism by Nigel Yates in 1999. On top of that, many of the early leaders of the Movement have been reassessed in a series of often substantial biographies. By examining some of the history, ideas and personalities of the Movement in the light of contemporary scholarship, this book also hopes to enable the modern reader to become sufficiently familiar with this significant phase of nineteenth-century church history that he or she can then confidently pursue further research into the more detailed and specialist areas.

1

Contexts

Where did the Oxford Movement come from, and how did it relate to other forces at work in both the Church and the State in the second quarter of the nineteenth century? Answers to these questions are not always straightforward, nor as obvious as they might appear to be at first sight. Clearly it did not suddenly arrive, fully formed, out of thin air, and in many ways it was much more a product of its times than even some of its modern historians have appreciated. In order to begin to understand this Movement, therefore, we shall have to start by examining the ecclesiastical background to it, and the conditions in which the Church of England found itself in the 1820s and the 1830s.

The Church of England and the Oxford Movement

Ever since the earliest years of the Reformation under Henry VIII there had been churchmen who had emphasized the continuity of the national Church with its pre-Reformation past. For one thing, the structure of Church order remained firmly built on bishops, priests and deacons, a deliberate link with the past which had been abandoned by most continental Reformers and Churches. However, a number of points need to be made about this. For the Oxford Movement the existence of continuing episcopal government in the national Church was a matter of the highest importance; the earliest of the *Tracts for the Times* centred on this concept of Apostolic Succession, the linking of the contemporary Church back to the Apostles themselves and hence to Christ, through the unbroken chain of their successors, the Bishops. But it is now clear that the Tractarians invested this with an importance, and interpreted it in a way, quite at odds with the English Reformers or those who followed them in the next centuries. As Kenneth Hylson-Smith has argued, the Reformers did not see the historic episcopate 'as of the essence of the church or as a vital component of her catholicity'.[1] Even in the seventeenth century the Caroline Divines, a group of theologians with whom the later Tractarians liked to compare themselves, refrained from any condemnation of Lutheran or Calvinist Churches on the continent which had departed from the practice of episcopacy.[2] And Charles I's Archbishop of Canterbury, William Laud, accepted the validity of continental Protestant orders.[3] Here, as in a number of other ways, the Oxford Movement introduced an emphasis that had not really existed among previous groups of High Churchmen.

This in itself raises a further issue concerning the continuity of a High Church tradition within the Church of England. While there were clearly groups and individuals who from the sixteenth century onwards appeared to share many ideas that collectively have become labelled 'High Church', modern research has begun to cast doubts on the concept of an unbroken tradition from the Reformers onwards. For instance, Richard Hooker (1554–1600), the author of the *Laws of Ecclesiastical Polity,* has often been seen as a pivotal figure in this supposed continuity, and John Keble himself edited Hooker in the nineteenth century, emphasizing this point. But in many ways to view Hooker in this light is 'an unwarranted retrospective interpretation', and to see him as part of 'a continuous, unbroken, ever-developing and growing or consistent High Church tradition' is incorrect.[4]

There was one specific group of churchmen, however, with whom the later Tractarians did have some affinity, and these were the Nonjurors. This group originated in the arguments surrounding the deposition of James II in 1688, and in his replacement by William III. Some nine bishops and about 400 other clergy refused to accept William on the grounds that by doing so they would break their previous oaths to James, and so departed from the Established Church to form a separate ecclesial body. In 1694 they began consecrating their own line of bishops, a practice they continued well into the eighteenth century. However, by the latter part of that century their numbers were declining, and they eventually became absorbed back into the mainstream national Church. But perhaps because they were free from the constraints of the Establishment, they developed in some ways that were similar to the later Tractarians in their emphasis on the essential nature of episcopacy, their stress on the spiritual independence of the Church from the State, and their tentative negotiations with the Eastern Orthodox Churches. Yet even the Nonjurors retained a loyalty to the Reformation, and a reluctance to accept more Catholic doctrines such as the Real Presence of Christ in the Eucharist, that still largely separate them from the Tractarians.[5]

But any real concept of a continuous High Church tradition before the advent of the Oxford Movement can only realistically be traced to the middle of the eighteenth century. As Peter Nockles has argued, the accession of George III in 1760 was crucial in transforming High Churchmen from a politically beleaguered minority into a privileged group for whom the 'tide of ministerial preferment turned'; by the 1790s the whole character of the episcopate was changing, and by the 1830s and 1840s there were more High Churchmen on the episcopal bench than at any time since 1688.[6] At the same time there emerged a distinctively High Church group in some ways comparable to the better-known Evangelical Clapham Sect; this was the Hackney Phalanx, part of a 'discreet and restrained revival of High Church divinity'.[7] This group of perhaps 50 to 100 clergy and laity has not received the attention from modern historians that their obvious influence in the early nineteenth century deserves.[8] However, Nockles has shown that from the end of the Napoleonic Wars in 1815 to the death of Lord Liverpool in 1827 the Phalanx exerted a huge influence on episcopal and other church appointments largely through their 'bishop-maker', H. H. Norris, and his association with the Tory Prime Minister.[9] But with Liverpool's death in 1827, rapidly followed by the repeal of the Test and Corporation Acts in 1828, Catholic Emancipation in 1829, and the arrival of a new Whig-dominated government in 1830, the Phalanx was thrown into confusion and their influence rapidly waned. As the decade of the 1830s opened, High Churchmanship as anything resembling an organized and effective party was in disarray. Into this vacuum stepped the Tractarians. The emergence of the Oxford Movement must therefore be seen 'in the context of the decline of Hackney'.[10] But, as we shall also see when we come to examine the distinctive beliefs of the Tractarians, the latter's relationship to High Churchmen was as much one of fracture as continuity.

Part of the reason for that lay in the Oxford Movement's view of the Georgian Church. It very rapidly became an article of faith among Tractarians, and emphasized repeatedly in their rhetorical literature, that the eighteenth century had been a long period of decay and neglect from which they, the Tractarians, were now uniquely rescuing the Church. The Tractarian theologian, Robert Wilberforce, succinctly encapsulated this viewpoint [Document 3]. In that theory there was little room to give credit to the labours of Hackney and other High Churchmen of the Georgian period. As Newman wrote imperiously in the Advertisement to the first collection of the early *Tracts* in 1834, doctrines which he claimed had been held in the Church of England in the more distant past 'at present have been obsolete with the majority of her members, and are withdrawn from public view even by the more learned and orthodox few who still adhere to them'.[11] But even if we just consider that supposedly Tractarian rediscovery of the Apostolic Succession, there had been a continual stream of works on the subject by High Churchmen from the 1760s to the 1820s.[12] Not for the first or last time we shall see that there is sometimes a gulf between Tractarian rhetoric and actual reality.

This also extends to the repeated Tractarian claim that their Movement was directly related to, and a contemporary revival of, the work of the Caroline Divines. These were the bishops and other writers who flourished in the reigns of James I, Charles I and their Stuart successors in the seventeenth century, and which is often seen as the 'classic' period of Anglican apologetics. But what is equally clear is that the Tractarians were far from alone in asserting their descent from, or affinity with, the Carolines. Here was another source of tension with the existing High Churchmen who also claimed that they represented the genuine 'Laudean party'.[13] On top of that, while many of the *Tracts* consisted of lengthy passages from the Caroline Divines and the Movement published a systematic collection of their works in the *Library of Anglo-Catholic Theology*, giving the impression that their beliefs were grounded in those of the earlier men, again in reality the Tractarians in general, and especially Newman in particular, often quoted in a highly selective manner from their works.[14] Bishops in their Charges, High Church writers, and Evangelicals at the time, all pointed repeatedly to this Tractarian rhetorical device, most developed by Newman and taken to its most extreme in his *Tract 90* in 1841, of quoting passages from the Caroline Divines which suited their controversial purposes but conveniently ignoring other passages which did not.[15]

The conclusions of modern research are therefore at variance with the Tractarians' own understanding of their relationship to the Anglican past in the form of a continuing or revived tradition of High Churchmanship, and to that understanding so uncritically accepted by the early historians of the Movement. To see them as the lineal descendants of groups such as the Caroline Divines or even the Nonjurors, while at the same time largely ignoring or dismissing a consistent Georgian High Church tradition, is to make a double error of interpretation. The Tractarians only related themselves to the past history of their Church in ways which suited their contemporary controversial purposes. Until relatively recently it has been the Tractarian view that has become part of the Movement's mythology perpetuated by the predominance of sympathetic historians. What is now emerging is a view of the Tractarians as at least as much innovators as revivalists. As this study progresses, that view will sharpen its focus. Looked at from this perspective, the Oxford Movement, as it gained momentum and developed its concepts in the 1830s and 1840s, represents one of the most fundamental *discontinuities* in the history of Anglicanism. It is as much a new beginning as it is an inheritance from the past. And so to begin to answer the question of where the Movement came from by uncritically linking it to previous groups of individuals is at best only to offer a very limited answer, and at worst to distort not only the history of Tractarianism but also Anglicanism itself.

If an examination of earlier High Churchmanship cannot fully answer the question about the origins of the Oxford Movement, then other sources must be examined. Among these is the relationship of the Movement to the Evangelical reawakening which began in the mid-eighteenth century. It has always been a matter for comment by historians of the Movement that some of its first leaders came to Tractarianism via Evangelicalism, including Newman himself, and among his friends at Oxford, Robert and Henry Wilberforce, the sons of the great Emancipator, and Henry Manning. Yet the exact relationship of Evangelicalism to Tractarianism has always been open to different interpretations. One key issue, given his dominant role in the Movement, has always been the genuineness of Newman's conversion experience at the age of fifteen. In his *Apologia* Newman publicly revealed details of this, but Evangelicals then told him that they did not recognize this as a true conversion experience within their tradition. Some scholars agree with them, notably Martin J. Svaglic, the editor of the modern edition of the *Apologia*, and also one of Newman's most recent biographers, Sheridan Gilley.[16]

Be that as it may, on the broader issue of whether or not Tractarianism was the continuation or fulfilment of the earlier movement, there remain a variety of opinions. One of the few of the early Tractarians to write explicitly about this was Robert Wilberforce who was clear that 'the second movement was a sort of consequence of the first'.[17] Gladstone, the Tractarian sympathizer, was equally in agreement with this viewpoint, and by 1897 it had become enshrined in the mythology of the Movement as reflected in the sympathetic historical account by J. H. Overton.[18] Clearly these interpretations should be treated with some caution in the light of what has been said already about the Tractarians' view of themselves. From the Evangelical perspective, however, there has always existed an equal desire to distance their own revival from the later one; so in 1933 Bishop E. A. Knox's account of the Movement contained an explicit statement that to see the Tractarians as a continuation or an outcome of the Evangelical movement was one of several 'popular misconceptions'.[19] While it may be possible to argue that Knox was writing at a time when scholarship could still be influenced by Church party allegiance, that criticism certainly could not be levelled at the modern account of the Evangelical response to the Tractarians by Peter Toon. He carefully chronicles a much more complex and subtle relationship between the two revivals, beginning with a wary interest from the Evangelicals and clear desire on Newman's part to harness them to the cause of the Oxford *Tracts*. From the earliest days of the Movement he was writing letters to, and articles for, the Evangelical periodical the *Record*.[20] Individual Evangelicals also expressed clear sympathy with the new ideas from Oxford, including men of such eminence as Bishop Sumner of Winchester.[21] Tractarians, High Churchmen and Evangelicals joined together in common cause on a number of vital ecclesiastical and university controversies right up until 1836.[22] But Toon then describes how this early harmony began to slowly disintegrate, with the first substantial Evangelical attack on the Tractarians appearing in the *Christian Observer* in 1837.[23] From then onwards the relationship rapidly turned to outright hostility on the part of most Evangelicals, and by 1840 the two movements were clearly separated into opposing camps.[24] Toon is clear that the reasons for the breach were theological. As the Tractarians developed their ideas during the 1830s and 1840s it seemed as if all the classic battles of the Reformation would have to be re-fought, from the nature of the Church and her ministry, to Justification and the Sacraments.[25]

11

However, there is another school that tends to look beyond the narrower theological disputes between the two movements and instead stresses the 'indirect, more or less paradoxical, connections.'[26] As early as 1934 Yngve Brilioth identified Methodism, Anglican Evangelicalism and the Oxford Movement as the English components of a wider Pietistic reaction against the rationalism of the Enlightenment.[27] This line of argument was repeated by Dieter Voll in 1963, but, tantalisingly, neither really developed their ideas in any substantial form. However, it was clearly their overt desire for holiness and the obvious enthusiasm of the early Tractarians that blew like a refreshing wind through the dry formalism of the older High Church Party that so attracted many young Evangelicals; they saw in the new revival the same charismatic fire that had first drawn their fathers and grandfathers to a deeper level of commitment to their faith in previous generations. In his 1842 Bampton Lectures the Evangelical, James Garbett, acknowledged the 'deep chord' that the Tractarians had struck, buried inside so many[28] [Document 4].

But that spiritual empathy alone would not account for the attractiveness of the Oxford Movement to those whose first experience of Christianity had been within the Evangelical fold. As we did with the older High Churchmen, so we must also do here and seek clues in the state and condition of Evangelicalism in the 1820s and 1830s. In some ways both Hackney and Clapham shared a similar malaise as the second quarter of the century began. The Hackney Phalanx was not only thrown into confusion by the constitutional upheaval that opened in 1828, but also it signally failed to attract the rising generation to what increasingly came to be seen as a group of 'ponderous old men'.[29] At the same time the Evangelical party was losing its greatest figures, William Wilberforce dying in 1833, and Charles Simeon, its most prominent force in Cambridge University, in 1836. As David Newsome has written:

> The Evangelical party lost its greatest leaders, and failed to secure the services of those who should have been their natural successors ... at the precise moment when the battle between Church and State, and between Christianity and infidelity, looked to be at its fiercest.[30]

Neither High Church nor Evangelicals seemed able to offer a message of defiant hope at this moment of profound crisis. For many it was the brilliant young men from Oxford who sounded the authentic call to arms, in a language that resonated in an almost-forgotten way in the hearts of Churchmen of all parties. Not for nothing the Tractarians chose as the motto that is printed on the title page of the bound volumes of the *Tracts,* the urgent question of St Paul: 'If the trumpet give an uncertain sound, who shall prepare himself to the battle?'[31] They believed they had the answer.

The Church in danger

It is now often very difficult for students of the nineteenth-century Church to appreciate the watershed that is represented by the five years from 1828 to 1833. The Established Church faced its most severe crisis since the time of the Civil War, as many of the foundations upon which it had been built seemed to be disintegrating beneath it. Links between itself and the State that had appeared as natural points of mutual sustenance for generations were not only being called into question by enemies without, but also increasingly abandoned by friends within. Yet at the same time it is not always clear from historical accounts of the Church in this period that there is a wider context in which these particular battles were being waged. The Church of England was not alone in her plight.

The years after 1815 saw a revival in a more intense way of the demands for reform of Church and State which had first been voiced in the closing decades of the previous century. The long years of war with France had both inhibited the progress of reform and at the same time established the fear of a connection between religious and political dissent. But during these years the nature of English society had been changing as well from the double impact of nascent industrialization and unprecedented urban expansion. And in these growing towns and cities it was largely religious dissent, both in the form of the new Methodism and reinvigorated older sects, that was proving more successful than the Established Church. The growth of Protestant dissent, in wealth as well as numbers, was something which the government could not ignore indefinitely. Three times between 1787 and 1790 attempts to repeal the hated Test and Corporation Acts had failed in Parliament. With the return of peace in 1815 fresh campaigns were not long delayed to persuade a reluctant government of the wisdom of this move. And then there was Ireland. Rebellion in 1798 led not only to the Union of 1801 but also almost brought political emancipation for its majority Catholic population as well, frustrated only by the intransigence of George III and the resignation of Pitt. For some in the governing elite in England after 1815 it increasingly looked as if the prudent course would be to grant full political rights to the swelling religious minorities rather than have them taken by force.[32]

But the Church of England was not the only institution subjected to assault by radicals in these years. Pressures to bring about the removal of what is usually termed the confessional state were themselves enfolded within a much wider movement for the wholesale dismantling of the *ancien régime*. The radical Unitarian John Wade had first produced his *Black Book* in 1820, and this had gone through a series of expanding editions culminating in the *Extraordinary Black Book* of 1831–2. This volume was among the most infamous and detailed records of all that was in his view corrupt in the British State. In its final form it ran to over 670 pages of statistics and narrative. However, while he gave pride of place to an assault on the Established Church, its patronage, its pluralist and non-resident clergy, its inequitable distribution of its vast wealth, and its general moral failings, this tirade only occupied the first 182 pages. The rest of the book launches into similar attacks on the Crown and its revenues and Civil List, the aristocracy, the legal system, the taxation system, the Bank of England, the municipal corporations, and the House of Commons, among others. For Wade, as for other dissenters and radicals, the Established Church was only one part, albeit a key one, of a much larger system of corruption and neglect. To put it another way, the Established Church's pluralist and non-resident clergy were but the ecclesiastical equivalent of Parliament's Rotten Boroughs. However exaggerated or inaccurate some of Wade's claims might have been, their impact was undoubted.[33] Something of the flavour of his attacks, typical of the radical campaign can be gleaned from these extracts [Document 5].

For the clergy of the Established Church whether Evangelical, High, or of no fixed party allegiance, the prospects implied by radical reform seemed earth-shattering. For centuries there had been explicit links between their ecclesiastical body and the State, given its first detailed statement by Hooker. Repeal of the seventeenth-century Test and Corporation Acts would, it was feared, flood the chamber of the House of Commons with religious dissenters; emancipation would do the same for Catholics. The previously Anglican purity of Parliament would be violated. The authority of The Book of Common Prayer, for instance, rested upon its status as a document sanctioned by the lay synod of the

14

Church: Parliament. What would Dissenters and papists do to the Church's liturgy once allowed entrance to the legislature? Even if in reality the more extreme fears were not realized, then still the even more potent symbolism of their presence would be sufficient violation of ancient assumptions. And once the breach was made the floodgates of reform would be opened, sweeping away every privilege from tithes and church rates to the Anglican exclusivity of the universities of Oxford and Cambridge themselves.

In 1828 the Tory government, ministers of which were supposed to be the Church's friends and defenders, finally repealed the Test and Corporation Acts and from that point onwards the crisis developed. As civil war loomed in Ireland, the following year they compounded their sins by passing Catholic Emancipation, seeming to renege on past promises. 1830 saw the collapse of the decades-long Tory grip on Parliament and a Whig-led government came in, pledged to widespread reform. They turned first to the House of Commons itself, and after two years of fierce battle in which the bishops, the beneficiaries of Tory patronage, largely sided with the opposition to reform, the great Bill was finally passed. Next, the Whigs trained their reforming guns on the Church. In February 1833, the Irish Church Temporalities Bill was introduced into Parliament. It proposed the abolition of two of the archbishoprics and eight other bishoprics of the Church of Ireland, with consequent savings of £150,000 a year. To some, reducing the scale of a Church that claimed the allegiance of barely a tenth of the Irish population seemed both rational and equitable. But for many of the clergy of a Church by law established not only in England and Wales but in Ireland too, this appeared to be but the first attack on their privileges. It was on 14 July that John Keble, the Professor of Poetry at Oxford, climbed into the pulpit of the University Church to preach the sermon at the service which opened the assizes. He chose as his subject 'National Apostasy'; for some the Church's counter-attack had begun at last.[34]

Others, however, were less convinced of the Church of England's capacity either theologically or morally to mount such a campaign successfully. One of those was Thomas Arnold, then the Headmaster of Rugby School, and already noted for the liberalism of his theology. In a memorable comment he remarked: 'The Church, as it now stands, no human power can save.'[35] Arnold was merely voicing the hopes and fears of many both within and outside the Established Church. Not surprisingly the early 1830s saw a number of proposed schemes and plans for the reform of that Church, one of the most notable being that of Lord Henley produced in 1832. In the January of the following year Arnold published his own *Principles of Church Reform* which went through no fewer than four editions in the space of six months.[36] Unlike Henley, Arnold did not advocate disestablishment or a re-distribution of the Church's property, but instead looked for a redefinition of the Establishment by means of inclusion. For him the doctrinal differences between the Church of England and the Dissenters were of secondary importance. Thus the Establishment could be saved and revitalized by finding ways to bring them in to it. All but Roman Catholics, Quakers and Unitarians, believed Arnold, could be accommodated within this new model of a national Church, tolerating a wide divergence in belief and practice, and thus removing the need for any religious tests for entry to the great institutions or offices of Church and State. Once within the Establishment the former dissenters would then play a significant role in an internal reorganization of its more venerable aspects. The problem for Arnold was one, therefore, largely of politics and rationality; religious beliefs, beyond certain basic concepts, were not the main issues of contention [Document 6].

The Oxford Movement: conservative or radical?

How did the emerging Oxford Movement fit into this conflict between the opposing forces of conservatism and radicalism? Many modern historians seem to be as perplexed about this as some Churchmen had been in the 1830s. On the one hand, it seems clear that a movement that sought to uphold what it saw as the traditional structures and beliefs of an institution as ancient as the Church of England, and defended them by reference to its past, whether in the form of the Caroline Divines or the Fathers of the even remoter fourth and fifth centuries, was a force very much on the side of conservatism. Thus William Gibson can argue that the Oxford Movement 'took on the form of a reactionary rearguard defence of episcopacy and apostolic government' and that its traditional beliefs were the very 'touch stone of reaction'.[37] Froude's biographer, Piers Brendon, echoes these views: 'It was determinedly retrogressive in an age of reform', he writes of the Movement.[38] Kenneth Hylson-Smith agrees:

[The] movement can, with hindsight, be seen, at least in its

16

church-state aspect, as an attempt to resist irresistible change, and an heroic defence of an ideal which belonged to a former age and to circumstances which had passed, never to return.

He sees it as a movement which fundamentally 'tended to look backwards'.[39] Yet a few pages later the same writer can speak of 'the innovative progressive nature of the Oxford Movement' in contrast to the older High Churchmen.[40] As David Newsome has noted: 'the Tractarians were not always backward-looking; not wholly devoid of the gift of prophecy'.[41] And Piers Brendon interprets the influence of Froude on the Movement in a strikingly different way: 'Froude's ideal was a radical Church founded on Catholic truth. His achievement was to draw dramatic attention to the incongruity of a conservative Church resting, partially at least, on a revolutionary base.'[42] George Tavard has also pointed to this same incongruity in Newman and an Oxford Movement that from its very beginnings 'contained revolutionary elements'. Of Newman, Tavard noted: 'There is something ironical in the fact that he, who politically and socially was reactionary, should have finally bowed to a religious revolution which he had nurtured in spite of his first intentions.'[43] What is one to make then of a Movement, one leader of which, Newman, when returning from his Mediterranean journey in 1833 refused to look on a tricolour on a vessel in Algiers because of its association with all things revolutionary, while another leader, Froude, wrote home from that same journey at almost the same time: 'When I come home I mean to read and write all sorts of things, for now that one is a radical there is no use in being nice'?[44]

One way of understanding, if not resolving, the problem of a phenomenon that appears to be both conservative and radical at the same time is to do what few writers on the nineteenth-century Church, and specifically on the Oxford Movement, have done, and that is to draw some comparisons between the ecclesiastical world of the 1830s and the political, social and economic spheres in the same decade. When one does so, what becomes strikingly clear is that the combination of conservatism and radicalism within the same individuals and movements was actually very much a characteristic feature of the decade and at the root of much of the social reform of the period. Take, for instance, the case of the new textile factories. In 1830 a furious letter had first appeared in the *Leeds Mercury* with the deliberately provocative title of 'Yorkshire Slavery'; its author, Richard Oastler, was a Tory and an Evangelical, and in the letter he compared the child labour he had recently seen in the worsted mills of Bradford to the black slavery of the West Indian sugar plantations. Oastler's letter played a similar role to Keble's Assize Sermon in initiating what became a powerful movement for the reform of the factories. What is of even greater interest here, however, is that Oastler and the other leaders of this movement were as conservative and traditional in their Toryism as any of the leaders from Oxford. But at the same time they initiated a movement of clearly radical reform, and indeed joined forces with many working-class radicals to give birth to a phenomenon usually called 'Tory Radicalism'.[45] At the same time they also shared with the Oxford clerics a deep loathing for Robert Peel's brand of Liberal Toryism, which sought to accommodate traditional Toryism with the new economic theories of Liberalism and political economy. Michael Sadler, the MP who introduced the Bill for factory reform into Parliament in 1832, called Liberal Toryism 'earthly, selfish, and devilish', language worthy of any Tractarian.[46] Then in 1834 the Whigs reformed the Poor Law in ways that again many traditional Tories saw as an abandonment of age-old values and a hopeless compromise with the forces of economic Liberalism. When the consequent reorganization of the workhouses reached the northern mill towns in 1836, Oastler and his friends and allies were ready and a new movement of Tory Radical protest flourished in 1837 and 1838.[47]

In what ways, then, can the Tractarians be described as radical? A number of points stand out here, some of which will be explored in more detail in the next chapter, but two surround the concepts of Establishment and authority in the Church of England, and of the position of the clergy in particular. The Tractarian leaders quickly appreciated the implicit dangers to the Church in the changed relationship between it and the State following the constitutional developments of 1828–33, and the possible benefits of a separation between the two as a result. As Froude wrote in 1834:

> The body of the English nation either are sincere Christians or they are not: if they are, they will submit to Discipline as readily as the primitive Christians did. If not, let us tell the truth and shame the devil: let us give up a *national* Church and have a *real* one.[48]

As early as 1829 Keble had seen positive advantages in a separation writing that: 'I am now, and have been for some time, convinced that the spiritual advantages enjoyed by ourselves and our charges at present are much greater than we have reason to expect, humanly speaking, if we were separated from the State.'[49] Newman echoed these views in 1833 when he commented to a correspondent: 'For myself I agree with you in wishing the Church loose from the tyranny of the state, but should not yet like to say so in print.'[50] Perhaps the nearest they did come to saying this in print was in 1835 in Froude's *Tract* number 59: 'Church and State', in the opinion of his most recent biographer 'the most cogently argued and trenchantly expressed case against Erastianism, particularly as it threatened the Church in the changed conditions of the 1830s'.[51] In this *Tract* Froude draws up lists of both the positive and negative aspects of Establishment; among the former is the protection of law enjoyed by the Church, its right to raise a church Rate, and its bishops to sit in Parliament. But he sees the disadvantages as more potent and immediate and devotes far more space to them; the two chief being lay patronage and state interference in the Church's discipline.

The other radical view of the Tractarians concerned the clergy, and specifically their social status as 'gentlemen'. In the very first of the *Tracts* in 1833 Newman had criticized too many of the clergy for resting their authority over their flocks on a number of secular advantages such as superior birth, education and wealth; in 1834 Froude wrote in a similar vein from the West Indies when discussing the potential education of a black clergy. He pointed out that St Paul had maintained himself by the lowly occupation of tent-making and still discharged the duties of an apostle, and added: 'the notion that a priest must be a gentleman is a stupid exclusive Protestant fancy, and ought to be exploded'.[52] In place of both the support of the State and the 'gentleman heresy' the Tractarians proposed an alternative spiritual and sacramental foundation for the authority of the Church and its clergy.

Thus, in their own specifically ecclesiastical mixture of the intensely conservative with the potentially frighteningly radical, the leaders of the Oxford Movement were very much of their times and shared concepts and ideas in common with many others in the 1830s. Far from being no more than typical backward-looking reactionaries, they were often, as David Newsome argued, prophetic in placing before the Church a vision of itself which presented to the world of the 1830s and 1840s a model of a national Church in many ways far more original and practical than that advocated by Liberals like Thomas Arnold.

Cultural contexts

The hundred years from the middle of the eighteenth to the middle of the nineteenth century saw the most fundamental shifts in the European intellectual and cultural spheres since the Renaissance. The emergence and flowering of Romanticism affected the whole of Western civilization but it is notoriously difficult to pin down in a few sentences as it has 'something intrinsically and astonishingly complex' about itself.[53] Yet certain themes were clearly central to most of the manifestations of Romanticism in this period. At its heart was a rejection of some of the fundamental concepts of the Enlightenment, which themselves in part go back to the Renaissance, and chief among these were the Romantics' belief that the feelings, the intuition, and above all the power of imagination inherent in mankind were on an equal footing with the intellect and reason so adored by the rationalists of the Enlightenment in the pursuit of truth. Poetry was as valid as scientific enquiry in the attempt to fathom the mysteries of the universe. At the same time the Romantics revolutionized the way that nature and the past were viewed. Natural phenomena were no longer reduced to a set of discoverable scientific laws, but elevated to objects of wonder and devotion which could inspire the human spirit; in the same way the Enlightened distaste for historical periods such as the Middle Ages as sunk in barbarism and superstition was replaced by the Romantics as centuries full of the exotic and even the grotesque but through which the spiritual in mankind had been expanded. This was reflected in architecture where the form and symmetry of Classicism gave way to a building style inspired by the Middle Ages, the Gothic, in which the full extent of the imagination and individuality of mankind could be expressed. Indeed, this emphasis on the individual, often seen as the introspective genius, was another Romantic departure from the past. One form the individual could also take was that of the heroic victim who audaciously championed the truth in a hostile world.[54] As Shelley was to write of poets, they are

> Cradled into poetry by wrong;
> They learn in suffering what they teach in song.[55]

It has long been recognized that the Oxford Movement emerged in a world in which Romanticism had come to its maturity, and that this cultural revolution represented one of the most potent influences on the first Tractarian leaders. As Stephen Prickett wrote in 1976: 'The Oxford Movement was a religious flowering of the English Romantic Movement', an opinion repeated more recently by Aidan Nichols: 'In a sense Tractarianism was the ecclesial form of the Romantic Movement in England, something indicated by the association with it of the main Romantic poets'.[56] And the man who first mediated the influence of those Romantic poets not only to the Oxford Movement in particular but also to the Church of England in general was John Keble. At a time when many Churchmen were still suspicious of poets like Shelley or Byron, more than tinged with political subversion and religious infidelity, it was Keble who channelled many of the ideas of the Romantics into the mainstream of English religious thought. It was as an undergraduate that Keble first read the poetry of the Romantics, and above all Wordsworth, and became a life-long admirer of the Lakes poet.

In 1827 he published *The Christian Year*, a collection of poems, Wordsworthian in feeling, based around the liturgical calendar of the Church of England. He composed a poem for each Sunday and holy day, prefaced by a verse from one of the biblical readings for that particular day. This volume became one of the most popular books of Victorian England and remained in print for half a century, selling an average of 10,000 copies a year, and made Keble a household name even before his participation in the Oxford Movement. In his poems Keble drew on the Romantic concepts of nature and imagination, but directed the hearts of his readers through these to the spiritual and the divine. As Geoffrey Rowell has commented in his perceptive essay on Keble the poet: 'Keble's world is God's creation, a sacramental universe, speaking to those who read it with the eye of faith of the pattern of God's being and activity.'[57] Here, in the opening verses of his poem for the Twenty-Third Sunday after Trinity, Keble uses the pattern of the seasons as the natural type of the Christian doctrine of death and resurrection [Document 7]. In seeking in his own words from the Advertisement to the original edition to bring 'thoughts and feelings into more entire unison with those recommended and exemplified in the Prayer Book', Keble was not doing something particularly original; however, what was new was the way he sought to do this, 'within an *emotional* context that was quite new to the Established Church', and which set him apart from both the older High Churchmen and the newer Evangelicals.[58]

Keble, however, was certainly not the only Tractarian influenced by Romantic sensitivities, nor indeed the only poet of the Movement. Newman and Froude, Isaac Williams and Robert Wilberforce all composed poems, and in 1836 a collection of Tractarian poetry was published under the title *Lyra Apostolica*. Among these poems was perhaps Newman's most famous lines, written in 1833, on an orange boat becalmed in the Mediterranean, frustrating him from returning to England after a desperate illness in Sicily, probably typhoid fever, which almost killed him. Newman poured into these verses all his thoughts and emotions at that critical moment in his life. He believed that God had spared him for a purpose and that renewal of vocation is reflected in the poem. He sees the pillar of fire that had led Moses through the desert to the Promised Land now illuminating his way as he returns to help the Church out of its and his 'encircling gloom'. But it also refers to what he had moaned to his Italian servant in his delirium, 'I have not sinned against the light'. The second verse may be seen as a recantation of his flirtation with the rationalism of the Liberal theologians in the late 1820s, which he sees as a manifestation of intellectual pride. Finally, he achieves his Promised Land, the 'angel faces' that he remembered so vividly from his childhood in his beloved home in Ham, in the words of Marcel Proust, realizing that 'the true paradises are the paradises we have lost'. Here Newman's Romantic imagination and personal introspection combined with his spiritual sensitivity to produce verses that spoke to many of his contemporaries and to become one of the most popular hymns of Victorian England[59] [Document 8].

This sense of the natural leading into the supernatural was not only found among Romantics like Coleridge, and in the religious poetry of the Tractarians, but was also at the root of sacramental theology.[60] The water of baptism washed away sins, and the bread and wine of the Eucharist became the body and blood of Christ. And it was in the liturgical performance of these rites that the veil separating this world from the next was most nearly lifted in the view of the Tractarians. The evolution of Tractarian Eucharistic theology will be explored in more detail in the next chapter, but in this sermon of Newman's preached in 1838 we can begin to glimpse how the Romantic imagination and the powerful truth of feelings could reach their spiritual climax in the Eucharistic services of the Church [Document 9].

Conclusion

In attempting to answer the questions of where the Oxford Movement came from and why it took the form it did, we have to take account of how the Tractarians related to both the past and the present in which they found themselves. As we have seen, the relationship between the new Oxford Movement and Anglican history is not really quite as straightforward or as linear as the Tractarians and many of their historians would have us believe. Tractarianism is not just a 'revival' of traditional Anglican High Churchmanship; it owed much to this earlier tradition, often in more ways than it was itself prepared to acknowledge, but at the same time it clearly departed from many of the fundamental tenets of that tradition. In exploring the distinctive beliefs of the Oxford theologians the next chapter will bring into sharper focus many of these discontinuities. What was characteristic of Tractarianism was its novelty rather than its familiarity. It not so much revived as reinvented the Anglican past for polemical purposes, purposes of its own present. But it also grew out of crisis, or rather a number of almost simultaneous crises. Both traditional High Churchmanship and Anglican Evangelicalism had 'run out of steam' and 'lacked the power to move or inspire the new generation unaided'.[61] This weakening unfortunately coincided with the most profound political challenge that the Church of England had had to face for many generations. The whole basis of the relationship between the Established Church and the State and its people was changing rapidly; in what sense in these new circumstances was it still a National Church? Different models of this concept were being promoted in the early 1830s, and in a sense the Tractarian answer was but one variety on offer. But in other ways the Oxford Movement was unique in its proposed solutions, and in its combination of extreme conservatism and unprecedented radicalism it offered a heady vision to those who found its concepts attractive.

In their own ecclesiastical version of Tory Radicalism, as in their embracing of Romanticism, the Tractarians were very much of their times. Obviously the particular contribution of each individual, as well as the precise location in Oxford University, were also aspects of the contexts in which Tractarianism was born. But in the light of what has been discussed in this chapter we can now move on to see how the Oxford Movement developed its particular ideas in the 1830s and 1840s.

2

Ideas

What beliefs did the Tractarians hold that made them so distinctive in the history of the Church of England? As with the previous chapter, answers to such questions are again neither simple nor straightforward. For one thing, the theological concepts of the Oxford Movement were characterized by their dynamism; a Tractarian 'creed' did not emerge, fully formed, in 1833 or any other date. Many of the ideas of the Movement took years, and in some cases decades, to grow and mature. On top of that, individual Tractarians also shifted their ground over time, the most obvious example being Newman; but Keble, Pusey and others also changed or modified their views as the years passed. It is therefore very difficult to give a precise theological definition of Tractarianism. One way to begin to approach this, however, is comparative. What tended to make them stand out were the emphases or interpretations which they put on particular doctrines in comparison to their contemporaries, whether traditional High Churchmen, Anglican Evangelicals, Liberals or Dissenters. By seeing what exercised other parties about the Tractarians we can begin to get a picture of their unique position at the time and in the broader sweep of Anglican history.

The dissemination of ideas

Before embarking on a more detailed investigation of these Tractarian beliefs we shall first of all pause to consider how this new group of theologians began to propagate their ideas. Obviously the word 'Tractarian' is derived from the Movement's most notable publications, namely, the *Tracts for the Times*. On first encountering the bound volumes of this series the modern reader might be forgiven for finding them a rather curious collection of writings. For one thing they are hardly systematic in the flow of ideas from one *Tract* to the next; a *Tract* on the Apostolic Succession might be followed by one discussing changes to Prayer Book services, followed by one on Advent or another season of the liturgical year, and that followed by a discussion of fasting, then back to the Apostolic Succession, and then to passages from a seventeenth-century writer. In addition, the style of writing can change from one *Tract* to the next, not only because the author is different but also because the audience for whom he is writing might change from clerical to lay. One reason for this seeming confusion was the decision, largely Newman's, that the *Tracts* would be the products of particular individuals rather than an editorial committee. Indeed, after the rapid publication of the first four *Tracts* there was a pause of a month while Newman and the High Churchman, William Palmer, argued over this point, with Newman eventually emerging triumphant. This demonstrates the tensions between the older traditionalists and the emerging group of younger men. Palmer was never happy with this arrangement and made it clear in his own account of the early history of the Movement that he believed Newman's action 'constituted himself an independent head, and a leader of a new movement' that 'was introducing as an essential principle the most unbounded freedom of speculation'.[1]

This reveals one essential difference between the Tractarians and what we would now call other 'pressure groups' in the political, economic and social spheres at the time. The Chartists, for instance, had their Charter with its Six Points; the movement for the reform of the working conditions in the textile mills coalesced around a demand for a ten-hour day; the Anti-Corn Law League was a 'single issue' movement. But there is no Tractarian equivalent. Where is their statement of aims or objectives? As Newman realized, an attempt to produce such a statement would probably have been more disruptive than unifying in the initial stages of the campaign, and as we shall see in the next chapter, the attempt to produce a Declaration along with the High Churchmen was very rapidly sidelined by Newman and his friends. This in itself is at the heart of the problem of attempting a definition of Tractarian beliefs. They never issued one, and so the later historian has to attempt to construct this from a mass of source material very diffuse in its nature. But in the longer term it was probably vital in allowing Tractarianism to evolve in a number of directions, and not to be for ever trapped in the particular issues of the 1830s.

The *Tracts for the Times* also present other difficulties for the reader. Initially they were designed to be relatively short and cheap, ranging in length from a couple of sides up to twenty pages, and costing only 1d or 2d each. In this they were hardly original, as Evangelicals such as Hannah More in the 1790s had achieved fame with a similar series of *Cheap Repository Tracts*.[2] The later Tractarians poured out their literature at a phenomenal rate and completed 70 *Tracts* in the space of two years. But then in 1835 Dr Pusey produced three *Tracts* together, numbers 67 to 69, on baptism, which in their final form with all the notes ran to some 295 pages. The subsequent numbers 70 to 90 followed this pattern and were all much more substantial publications, number 81 being the longest, Pusey's collection of writings by previous theologians on the Eucharistic Sacrifice, and running to 450 pages. Not surprisingly, unlike the early *Tracts,* these final 20 were composed over a longer time span of five years from 1836 to 1841. Altogether, the final six bound volumes of the *Tracts* run to about 3500 pages.

The modern scholar who is perhaps most familiar with the *Tracts for the Times* is the Swede, Rune Imberg. Not only are the *Tracts* voluminous in length but many of them passed through several editions, sometimes as many as eight or ten editions for a single *Tract*. Imberg has completed the monumental task of tracing every edition of all of the *Tracts*.[3] By comparing the changes in the wording, the additions and the omissions, through the various editions, Imberg has made a valuable contribution to our understanding of the progressive development of Tractarian thought and we will be referring to this at a number of points in this study.[4] On top of that he has given some fascinating insights into the actual publication and distribution of the *Tracts*. For instance, although they began to appear in September 1833, it was not until April 1834 that the collective title *Tracts for the Times* was first used.[5] Indeed, numbers 71, 72 and 79 were given a variation of that, being named *Tracts for the Times against Romanism*.[6] At the same time the distribution of the *Tracts,* published initially in batches of 1000 or 1500 each, was often most precarious. Newman described in his *Apologia* how he personally distributed them in handfuls to clergy he met on his travels through the country.[7] It was again not until April 1834 that this problem was largely overcome when Rivingtons, a publisher of High Church literature, began to print editions with standard lay-outs and agreed to act as the official agent for their distribution.[8] However, sales of the *Tracts* remained relatively modest until the late 1830s. The years from 1838 to 1840 then saw an upsurge with a number of reprints of all the existing *Tracts*, culminating in 1841 with the most infamous of the whole series, number 90 by Newman on the Thirty-Nine Articles, the last of the *Tracts*, which passed through two editions in a single month, totalling some 10,500 copies. Altogether Imberg estimates that the total number of *Tracts* printed in the years from 1833 to 1841 came to about 750,000, a truly staggering figure for the period.[9]

What were the responses from those who first read the *Tracts*? From the mid-1830s onwards these tended to polarize along party lines. Sympathetic readers enthused about the positive impact they made acting as guides and reference points for them through the sea of confusion in which many Churchmen believed themselves to be floundering. Typical of this reaction was T. T. Carter, the future Tractarian Vicar of Clewer near Windsor, and the eventual founder of a Sisterhood in that parish [Document 10]. Others, however, were appalled by what they read in these new *Tracts*. In 1836 the highly respected Evangelical, Edward Bickersteth, gave voice to this feeling that the *Tracts* were examples of Popery opening 'another door to the land of darkness'[10] [Document 11]. Protestants outside the Establishment were equally hostile to the *Tracts*, and in 1842 the Methodist Conference formally issued its own *Wesleyan Tracts for the Times,* a series of ten *Tracts* attacking a range of Oxford Movement concepts from the Apostolic Succession to the nature of the sacraments. The first of these *Tracts* alone sold some 10,000 copies.[11] The *Tracts for the Times* were divisive, then, but Newman always believed that they would be. Given the nature of the years in which he lived, he saw no other possibility. He ends the first of the *Tracts* with a call to the clergy to 'choose your side', neutrality or abstinence from worldly politics he argues being 'impossible in troublous times'.[12] Tractarianism was a clarion call to rally to the truth, not an attempt to create bogus unity.

The *Tracts for the Times* were not the only means employed by the early Tractarian leaders to disseminate their ideas. It often amazes the modern student to discover the sheer volume of sermons that were published, and presumably read, in the nineteenth century, and they were another vehicle through which the Oxford Movement sought to spread its concepts. Alongside the *Tracts* Newman, for instance, regularly published volumes of sermons that he had preached in the University Church in Oxford in his capacity as vicar. These *Parochial and Plain Sermons* were re-issued in their present form in 1868, consisting of sermons preached between 1825 and 1843. They run to some eight volumes, contain 191 sermons in over 2700 pages, and are in many ways the companions to the *Tracts*. They are not to be confused with Newman's *University Sermons*, however; fifteen far more substantial and scholarly works dating from the years 1826 to 1843. The other leaders of the Movement in its early years also published their own volumes of sermons, and besides these they all wrote occasional polemical pamphlets, books and other works. Of special note among these is the posthumous *Remains* of Richard Hurrell Froude; he died of consumption, the modern tuberculosis, in 1836 at the age of 32, and as was common at the time when an individual died relatively young his friends would gather the miscellaneous and normally unpublished writings into a commemorative volume. This Newman and Keble did, publishing the first part in 1838, and the second in 1839. As we shall see in the next chapter, the four volumes of Froude's *Remains* were to mark something of a watershed or turning point in the early history of the Movement. His letters, journals and other writings came as a bombshell to some who had initially been sympathetic to the Tractarians; here was an Anglican clergyman and Fellow of an Oxford college who reviled the Reformation, adored the Middle Ages and its churches, and practised the ascetic devotions of Roman Catholic monks. How could this be comprehended or tolerated within what most still acknowledged as a Protestant Establishment? Samuel Wilberforce, the brother of the Tractarians Robert and Henry, had been growing uneasy with the direction the Movement had been taking, but as attacks on it mounted he was clear that this was 'all the fruit of the wretched folly of Froude's *Remains*', and like many before or since saw it as perhaps the most monumental error of judgement that Newman made.[13] But some modern historians argue that Newman knew exactly what he was doing in revealing the most private thoughts of his friend to public gaze.

Another method employed by pressure groups and others in the nineteenth century to propagate their views was the periodical journal. Just as the Anti-Corn Law League had its free trade ideas promoted in *The Economist*, so the most important of the Tractarian journals was the *British Critic*. This had originally been a journal of the traditional High Churchmen, but in 1838 the Tractarians took it over with Newman as editor and from then onwards it produced a stream of articles much more in sympathy with the more strident beliefs of the Oxford Movement.[14]

So, from the *Tracts for the Times* themselves, through hundreds of sermons, pamphlets, books, and from the 1840s novels as well, the Tractarians had a wealth of vehicles for propagating their views. The problem for the modern historian is to extract the essence of their beliefs from this luxuriant growth of literature.

The visible Church

The Oxford Movement had been born in the years from 1828 to 1833 when the Church of England had gone through the crisis of what many saw as her abandonment by the State. The first *Tracts* and other early writings by the leaders of the Movement were designed to present an alternative source of authority for the Church; indeed, the concept of authority was at the very heart of the Movement in its early months. Newman had posed the question to the clergy in stark terms in the first of the *Tracts*: 'on *what* are we to rest our authority, when the State deserts us?'[15] His answer in that *Tract* was the Apostolic Succession, the sacramental transmission of the authority Jesus had first given to his apostles, among which were the powers to forgive sins, teach, and celebrate the Eucharist, passed on through the centuries to the present generation of bishops. This, for Newman, was perhaps the keystone separating the Church of England from the Protestant Dissenters. The Church of England possessed this precious chain with its links unbroken by the Reformation that gave it a unique identity back through the Middle Ages to the early Church and the apostles themselves. To be 'the Church' in the fullest sense of the word, episcopacy and an episcopally ordained priesthood was essential. This was not just a matter of Church order or government; it went to the heart of the spiritual life of Christians, giving a guarantee to the validity of the sacraments, such as the Eucharist, through which the Church itself was spiritually enlivened.

In the second of the *Tracts*, entitled 'The Catholic Church', Newman expanded on these concepts in an important passage that is perhaps the nearest any Tractarian came to a statement of the Movement's beliefs at this point [Document 12]. Newman first distinguishes the secular functions of the State from the exclusively spiritual ones of the Church. The State can legislate to make teachers, soldiers or magistrates; it cannot legislate for sacraments.

Newman's point is a simple one. No State can create bishops and priests because this is the exclusive, sacramental possession of the Church, a gift given to it by Jesus Christ himself. Yet clearly the State has attempted just this in Ireland with its abolition of the ten bishoprics, an act committed by a Parliament no longer exclusively Anglican. Against this Newman in the second paragraph again outlines the alternative authority of a Church based upon its apostolic foundation. Newman and the other Tractarians were at pains to emphasize that this is a *visible* Church too; no fewer than three of the early *Tracts* were devoted to this concept (numbers 11, 20 and 47), and in a sermon preached in 1834 Newman again outlined what was meant by this term [Document 13].

So what was so distinctive in this Tractarian concept of spiritual authority based on a visible Church? First of all what separated the new Movement here from the older High Churchmen, and so alarmed the latter, was the distinction the Tractarians emphasized between the Church and the State. For High Churchmen the Establishment was a positive concept, Church and State linked in mutual support. Newman, and to a greater extent Froude, saw this link now as an impediment and a danger; for them the whole situation had been transformed by the constitutional revolution of 1828–33. Hence Froude's comments about giving up a 'national' Church in favour of a 'real one'.[16] It was the radicalism of this implicit disestablishment view of the Tractarians that made the older school so fearful.[17] For the Evangelicals, on the other hand, the greater perceived danger was in the Tractarian insistence on the visible Church, and the downgrading of its invisible nature, a Church of the elect known only to God.[18] As Peter Toon has summarized the Evangelical position: 'The invisible Church was taken to be the true Church of Christ and members of this Church, together with false professors of Christianity, were to be found in visible (parish) congregations.'[19] For Evangelicals entry to the true, invisible Church, was by God's election, not episcopally ordained priests performing sacramental rites. But while Anglican Evangelicals accepted the episcopal order of the Church as biblical in origin, the Dissenters did not even admit to that; for them the whole Tractarian concept seemed effectively to 'unchurch' them.

In seeking to present evidence for the truth of their concept of the Church the Tractarians here, as in so many other areas, turned to the first centuries of Christianity, the early Church, or primitive Church of antiquity as it was often then called. This was for a number of reasons. First of all it was the age of the Fathers, those great theologians who had had the task of working out the implications of the life and death of Jesus. They included men such as Athanasius and Augustine, Basil and Leo, who had battled against heretics to preserve and define the true Christian faith. Second, it was the period in which the fundamental tenets of that faith had been formed into a series of doctrinal statements, such as creeds, in a number of universally recognized Church Councils. And third, it was the period in which the Church itself was still undivided; only later in the Middle Ages did the Latin West and the Greek East go their separate Catholic and Orthodox ways. Thus the pronouncements from this period had a unique weight of authority behind them. In pointing to that, however, the Tractarians were not doing something that in itself distinguished them from other groups in the history of Anglicanism. The Caroline Divines of the seventeenth century had also appealed to antiquity in justification of their theological arguments, as had the Nonjurors, and the continuing High Church tradition up to the 1830s. But Tractarians, led by Newman, used the Fathers and antiquity in a radically different way to any previous Anglican tradition. For High Churchmen antiquity was used to corroborate the teachings of the Church of England in her formularies and the writings of her divines. For them the normative model of the true Church was the Reformed English one, and antiquity could be used to justify it in so far as antiquity was in agreement with Anglicanism. Newman completely reversed this. For Tractarians 'antiquity became an absolute standard and final court of appeal'.[20] Antiquity was the normative model of the true Church, and the Church of England was only a true Church in so far as she was in agreement with that model, but a model also 'of a living church that could be reproduced in the nineteenth century'.[21] That was the essential point. The contemporary Church of England contained within herself all that was implicitly necessary not only to be, but also to look like, the true Church, if only she would realize what she was, the modern living embodiment of the Church of the Fathers.

To that end, Newman used the historical record of the early Church in a blatantly rhetorical way. He made an imaginative connection between the early centuries of Christianity and the Church of England in the 1830s. As Stephen Thomas has commented: 'His image of an apostolic Church turned upon by a persecuting State, as the re-enactment of the fourth and fifth-century struggles against heresy, proposes a startling analogy between antiquity and the nineteenth century.'[22] In the fourth century the

Roman Emperor, Constantine, had ended the persecution of Christians and made their religion an accepted part of the Roman world, himself being baptised into this faith on his death bed, and summoning the first universal Council of the Church to Nicaea in 325, which issued its famous statement of the true faith. However, physical now gave way to intellectual persecution. The great heretic Arius, and his followers named Arians after him, refused to accept this Nicene formula and persuaded Constantine to accept instead a compromise based on their beliefs about the relationship of Jesus to God. The Bishop of Alexandria, Athanasius, now emerged as the champion of the true Nicene faith, and suffered periodic exile and harassment at the hands of the State. The drama of this contest between the might of the heretical Roman State and the weak but theologically and morally pure Athanasius grabbed Newman's imagination. His interest in the Fathers had first been stimulated by reading Milner's *History of the Church* in the years after his Evangelical conversion.[23] From the summer of 1828 Newman began a systematic reading of the vast works of the Fathers, and the first fruits of this labour came with his book *The Arians of the Fourth Century*, largely written in 1831–2 and finally published in 1834. Rhetoric is the art of persuasion, either verbal or literary, and in his *Arians* Newman announced his rhetorical purpose: to show how the persecuting State of the fourth century found its counterpart in the nineteenth. The book was 'a rhetorical thrust against his ecclesiastical and political opponents' in the English Church and State.[24]

In so doing Newman had not only Whig politicians and their Tory lackeys in mind, but also those clergy who were equally betraying the Church from the inside by their adoption of a theological liberalism parallel to the political and economic one. Chief among these was Thomas Arnold. For the other lesson that Newman drew from the fourth century was that the heresy of ancient times had its counterpart in the liberalism of the modern age. Newman effectively invented the application of the word 'liberalism' to theology; but what did he mean by this? In its political and economic use it meant the removal of artificial barriers to things such as trade, hence the desire to remove customs duties and above all the Corn Laws, and the equally artificial rule by one class appointed by the accident of birth rather than merit or ability. Its theological meaning is somewhat less precise, however. It meant rather more than just a 'free trade' in religious belief, although it clearly grew out of the Latitudinarianism of the eighteenth century, the view that since so much was uncertain in religion a degree of latitude should be allowed rather than a dogmatic approach. In his *Apologia* Newman defined liberalism as 'the anti-dogmatic principle and its developments'.[25] And at the end of the *Apologia* in a lengthy note Newman attempts a longer explanation, perhaps the key sentence of which is:

> Liberalism then is the mistake of subjecting to human judgement those revealed doctrines which are in their nature beyond and independent of it, and of claiming to determine on intrinsic grounds the truth and value of propositions which rest for their reception simply on the external authority of the Divine Word.[26]

Liberals such as Arnold, however, were learning from the Enlightenment and the Germans that history was the scientific study of evidence and were subjecting both the biblical record and the history of the Church to such scrutiny. For them everything from miracles to the statements of the Church Councils were purely human events and activities, the proof of the truth of them beyond human reasoning and therefore of little authority. Newman took a very different view. In 1841 he replied in a series of letters to *The Times* to an assertion by Sir Robert Peel at the opening of the Tamworth Reading Room that the old Tory philosophy of a confessional State was gone. As Newman remarked:

> Many a man will live and die upon a dogma: no man will be a martyr for a conclusion ... After all, man is not a reasoning animal; he is a seeing, feeling, contemplating, acting animal ... Life is for action. If we insist on proofs for everything, we shall never come to action: to act you must assume, and that assumption is faith.[27]

The Liberal Anglicans saw all of this as a Romanticized misuse of history, and the Oxford Movement as profoundly unhistorical in its approach.[28] But for Newman, Church history was more than a matter of science; it was the sacred record of a divinely inspired institution whose pronouncements carried an authority which could no more be touched by human reason than its sacraments could by politicians.

Newman thus saw in nineteenth-century liberalism the modern version of many great heresies that had afflicted the early Church. But he went further. He equated liberalism with modern popular

Protestantism and in *Tract* 73, *On the Introduction of Rationalistic Principles into Religion,* he argued that both 'were reducing the transcendent in divine revelation to human standards of judgement'.[29] The mistake, for Newman, was that both intellectual and emotional approaches to Christianity, the latter typical of Evangelical preachers, put human experience in the place of the divine.[30]

Thus in their use of church history, and crucially that of the early Church, the Tractarians represented something quite novel in Anglicanism. They looked to an authority at once remote in time but nearer in the shared conditions of State persecution and corrosive heresy. All through the middle years of the 1830s Newman again and again adopted this rhetorical device of using the patterns of the past as lessons for the present. Perhaps nowhere is this more explicitly stated than at the end of his *Arians* where he clearly draws the parallels and looks for his modern Athanasius to rise to rescue the Church of England. There is something of the Romantic hero about Athanasius for Newman, just as for Froude it was Thomas Becket, another exiled champion of the Church against a persecuting State who appealed to his particular imagination.[31] And there is more than a hint in Newman's case that he saw himself in the role of the modern Athanasius[32] [Document 14].

The Via Media

Antiquity, then, was the touchstone by which the Church of England would be judged. But in the mid-1830s Newman extended this principle to both Protestantism and Roman Catholicism. He erected a theory by which Anglicanism would at least implicitly be nearer to antiquity than either Rome or Geneva. This theory he called the '*Via Media*' and first articulated it in *Tracts* 38 and 41 in the summer of 1834. 'The glory of the English Church is, that it has taken the VIA MEDIA, as it has been called. It lies *between* the (so-called) Reformers and the Romanists', wrote Newman.[33] These two *Tracts* take the form of a dialogue between a genuine enquirer after the truth, 'Laicus', and his clerical teacher, 'Clericus'. Through these two voices Newman outlines a programme for a Church that has largely forgotten its inheritance. 'Can you point to any period of church history, in which doctrine remained for any time uncorrupted? Three hundred years is a long time. Are you quite sure we do not need A SECOND REFORMATION?' asks Clericus rhetorically.[34] His answer is clear: 'I receive the church as a messenger from CHRIST, rich in treasures old and new, rich with the accumulated wealth of ages.'[35] At last Laicus gets the message, and outlines for the reader Newman's argument that over the course of time the Church has added various statements about the faith, not to corrupt it but rather to combat the successive errors of heresies; concepts which had lain dormant but implicit within the original message [Document 15]. The problem with this line of argument was simply one of authority again. Many statements about Christian belief have been issued over the centuries; but some contradict others, so which is right? And who judges? This was hardly a new problem in the nineteenth century, as it had been at the heart of the disputes between theologians in the early Church, at the time of the division between East and West, and again at the Reformation. Attempts had been made in the past to find a rule by which the distinction between orthodox and heretical beliefs could be judged, perhaps the most famous example from antiquity being the so-called Vincentian Canon, named after St Vincent of Lérins who had died some time before 450. In his *Commonitorium* he had proposed the Latin formula: *quod ubique, quod semper, quod ab omnibus creditum est* ('what has been believed everywhere, always and by all'). Newman's task was to demonstrate that these words applied more accurately to the Church of England than to either Rome, which had made unwarranted additions to the faith, or Protestantism, which had made equally unwarranted subtractions from it. As always, the test would be the undivided voice of antiquity.

However, Newman's first attempt at a definition of the *Via Media* in the two *Tracts* was somewhat unsatisfactory and, on a careful reading, ambiguous in some of its terminology. There is a confusion about distinguishing between 'doctrines' and 'articles', different types of 'articles', and which are essential.[36] These arguments were subsequently continued by Newman in a lengthy and detailed correspondence with the Frenchman, the Abbé Jager. But again the whole matter became bogged down in complex linguistic and terminological discussions.[37] Finally, in 1836, Newman tackled the whole problem in his most substantial discussion of the *Via Media*, his *Lectures on the Prophetical Office of the Church viewed Relatively to Romanism and Popular Protestantism*. In this work Newman makes the distinction between two Traditions in the Church, the Apostolic and the Prophetic. The first is the unchanging deposit of the faith, and the second is the vast literature effectively constituting a commentary on that deposit; but the latter is not fundamental and contains different levels or degrees of credit.

However, despite all the energy and time that Newman devoted to this effort to construct a *Via Media* that demonstrated that the Church of England had, uniquely, found the 'golden mean' between the additions of Rome and the subtractions of Protestantism, the one person he never entirely convinced was himself. It was those nagging doubts that form the background to Newman's slow drift towards Rome. As Rune Imberg has demonstrated in his study of the progressive editions of the *Tracts,* there is evidence of a steady movement in a Romeward direction as each new addition either modifies the wording, or removes whole passages, critical of Rome in some of the key *Tracts.*[38]

But whatever Newman's personal views were, it is clear that the concepts and terminology used in the *Via Media* theory had a profound influence on the way different groups within the Church of England perceived the position of Anglicanism in relation to other Christians. Before the 1830s High Churchmen had been happy to call themselves and their Church both Catholic and Protestant; indeed, the terms were hardly used in the sense of party labels before the advent of Tractarianism. The Caroline Divines and the High Churchmen of the eighteenth century had both seen the Church of England as the home of moderation and a middle way between *extreme* forms of Protestantism on the one hand, and Romanism on the other. But as Peter Nockles has argued, the Tractarian *Via Media* was a new concept, 'a "middle way" between Protestantism *per se* and Romanism. This subtle shift in the place assigned to Anglicanism in the theological spectrum in effect forced High Churchmen to decide whether they were Protestant or Catholic.'[39] They could no longer be both, and the very words began to acquire that sense of absolute division typical of modern Anglicanism. At the root of this division was the failure of the Reformers of the sixteenth century to live up to the test of antiquity in the eyes of the Tractarians. Froude was the most openly critical of the Reformation in a way that no Anglican had been before him. 'You will be shocked by my avowal, that I am every day becoming a less and less loyal son of the Reformation', he wrote in 1834, and elsewhere went even further: 'Really I hate the Reformation and the Reformers more and more', adding: 'The Reformation was a limb badly set – it must be broken again in order to be righted.'[40] If such views surprised the older High Churchmen, they outraged the Evangelicals.[41] For the latter the Reformation with its emphasis on the Bible as the fundamental source of authority in Christianity represented not so much a deviation from the Fathers as a return to the pure form of the faith before the corruptions of the medieval Church. Many Evangelical writers in the 1830s and 1840s were at pains to argue that the Tractarians had misunderstood the Fathers, or had used them far too selectively. Thus William Goode maintained that the Fathers themselves had upheld the primacy of Scripture, that the Tractarians had misinterpreted the Vincentian Canon and issued his own collection of the writings of the Fathers to beat the Tractarians at their own game.[42] For Evangelicals the Church of England was a reformed Church very much within the Protestant camp.

Sacraments and ascetics

Antiquity was not only the standard by which the position of Anglicanism was to be judged in relation to Rome and Protestantism, it was also the model which the Church of England should follow in her liturgical and spiritual life. She was not only theoretically the modern embodiment of the early Church, but also that embodiment in practice. She should *look* like the early Church. But in the 1830s she was in reality but a sad and impoverished reflection of antiquity in the view of the Tractarians. The Church of England had the capacity to be the contemporary realization of the early Church, but she had yet to appreciate her true vocation. The Tractarians set out to teach her. And if she learnt their lessons in full, the consequence would be nothing less than a revolution in the way the English worshipped. For the early Church, at the heart of worship was the gathering of the faithful Sunday by Sunday, and holy day by holy day, around the altar for the celebration of the Eucharist, the re-enactment of the taking of bread and wine by Jesus at the Last Supper. For the Tractarians the ideal of Anglican worship should be a reflection of what they found in antiquity. Froude articulated this as early as 1834 in his *Essay on Rationalism*[43] [Document 16]. Yet as Froude was aware, at that date this remained but a distant dream. For most Anglican parishes the norm of Sunday worship was not the Eucharist, which was relegated to a handful of days in the year, normally the major feasts and popularly referred to as 'Sacrament Sunday'. Before there could be any change in this pattern, Anglicans would have to learn why this sacrament was so important; and to some extent the Tractarians would have to teach themselves first.

What often surprises the modern reader is how little there is in the *Tracts for the Times* about the Eucharist, given its centrality in Tractarian liturgical life. One explanation for this is that the Oxford Movement was itself on a lengthy journey of exploration to discover what was in the early 1830s still very much unknown territory. What did it mean when Jesus had described bread as his body and wine as his blood at the Last Supper? How could one material element become another? And what was the purpose? Such questions, and a host of ancillary ones, had exercised the minds of Christians almost from the time of the Last Supper itself, and arguments about these questions had been at the heart of the Reformation. By exploring them again, the Tractarians revived many of the oldest and bitterest debates within Christianity. But that revival did not take place overnight; the Tractarians only slowly, over more than two decades, came to evolve what was to be their understanding of why the Eucharist should be at the heart of the life of the Church.

In the 1820s there was little difference in the way the Eucharist was perceived among the various parties within the Established Church; the arrival of the Tractarians in the 1830s was to change that permanently. Prior to the Oxford Movement arguments about how Christ was present in the Eucharist revolved around concepts such as Receptionism, where the spiritual and moral worthiness of the person receiving the bread and wine were crucial, and no identity between Christ and the physical elements was accepted; Virtualism, which accepted a presence of Christ in the Eucharist, although not a physical one, but saw the bread and wine as more than symbolic and once consecrated become the body and blood of Christ in spirit, power and effect; and Memorialism which saw the bread and wine as no more than memorials of Christ's body and blood, no supernatural gifts being imparted by the sacrament.[44] Then about 1830 first Froude, followed by Newman and then Keble, began to shift away from such concepts and associate the presence of Christ much more with the actual material elements of bread and wine. This was partly from a growing understanding of the sacramental teaching of the early Church, but also from their revulsion from the rationalism of the liberals that sought reasoned explanations for everything, and their equally growing distaste for the Reformation and its teachings.[45] By 1836 Keble was clearly becoming sceptical about the reformed theology of the Eucharist.[46] However, while rejecting ideas flowing from the Reformation for some years the Tractarians were reluctant to offer any alternative explanation for *how* Christ was present in the bread and wine. A passage from one of Newman's sermons in 1832 illustrates these points [Document 17]. What concerned Newman and the Tractarians most in the 1830s were the spiritual and *moral* effects of Eucharistic grace rather than precise definitions of how this was accomplished. But by the end of that decade Tractarians were coming to realize that they would have to be more explicit in their teaching; as Newman remarked in a sermon of 1838, alongside the irreverence of rationalism 'there is also a holy and devout curiosity which all who love God will in their measure feel'.[47]

The major turning point for Tractarian Eucharistic theology came with the writings of Robert Wilberforce, probably the greatest systematic theologian nurtured by the Oxford Movement; as David Newsome has remarked of him: 'he systematised where system was badly needed'.[48] After the publication of his major work on the Incarnation in 1849, his brother-in-law, Henry Manning, wrote to him advising him to read more widely in the medieval Scholastic theologians like St Thomas Aquinas, and the sixteenth-century Jesuits.[49] The significance of this is in the shift from the Fathers of the undivided Church to the great Catholic theologians of later ages. Here Wilberforce found what he and the Tractarians had been looking for. For instance, he found a Latin terminology that gave a precise framework for him to work in; 'the *sacramentum*, the sign or outward part, the *res sacramenti*, the thing signified or inward part, and the *virtus sacramenti,* the blessing or effect of partaking' of bread and wine.[50]

In 1853 Wilberforce published the fruits of his research, *The Doctrine of the Holy Eucharist*, in which he argued that Christ's presence in the Eucharist is supernatural, sacramental or not perceived by the senses, but at the same time real and not merely symbolic. And above all that presence is precisely located in the bread and wine after priestly consecration, what he called a 'real objective presence' not dependent on the worthiness of celebrant and receiver.[51] And Wilberforce went further in asserting that the Eucharist was a sacrifice. Just as Christ the High Priest eternally intercedes for mankind before the Father in heaven through the merits of his own earthly sacrifice on the cross, so the Eucharistic worship of the Church is the counterpart to this heavenly liturgy, a real participation in the eternal mediation of Christ, offering his body and blood, the one sacrifice for sins. Thus the Church through its visible, sacramental life becomes for Wilberforce the extension of the Incarnation itself; the body of Christ is both what it is and what it offers. Here, then, was the very centre and meaning of the

Christian life itself. In Alf Härdelin's words:

> What Newman in 1830 thought to be the only acceptable sacrifice to God, namely, the self-offering of obedient worshippers, Wilberforce, two decades later, taught to be acceptable only as assumed in the body of Christ, sacramentally present, and offered up to the Father through His priests.[52] [Document 18]

It had taken over twenty years for the full Tractarian teaching on the Eucharist to emerge, but when it did it came 'as manna in the wilderness' to the Movement.[53] In his *On Eucharistical Adoration* Keble used similar terms to Wilberforce giving his seal of approval to the teaching.[54] But for traditional High Churchmen such views were a novelty, not to be found in the Caroline or even Nonjuror Divines.[55] But if these doctrines were novel for High Churchmen, they were yet another outrage for Anglican Evangelicals and Dissenters. In 1856 William Goode, a leading Evangelical theologian, published his two-volumed work *The Nature of Christ's Presence in the Eucharist* specifically to challenge the theology of Wilberforce and other Tractarians.[56] For him the idea that Christ's presence was in any way joined to the physical bread and wine not only challenged some of the central tenets of the Reformers, but also could not be shown by reference to the Fathers. The truth for Goode was that Christ's reception by communicants was spiritual, and the only means of receiving this grace was by faith.[57] And as far as Wesleyans were concerned, this Tractarian doctrine was but further confirmation of their identity with the dreaded teachings of Rome.[58]

For Tractarians, then, the Eucharist was the centre of Christian life, and it was meant to feed the Christian heart and lead to holiness. Indeed, this desire for holiness became one of the distinguishing features of the Oxford Movement, and at least initially another point of contact with the earlier Evangelical awakening. For Evangelicals the process of conversion should lead the reborn Christian to a life that proclaimed the new depth of faith. Newman's first published sermon, preached while he was under the influence of Evangelicalism, was entitled *Holiness Necessary for Future Blessedness,* and reflected one of the sayings of the Evangelical Thomas Scott, 'Holiness rather than peace', which Newman used to repeat to himself like a mantra after his 1816 conversion.[59] But as the Oxford Movement developed through the 1830s and

1840s what was notable was not so much the similarities as the growing divergence with Evangelicalism. In the *Remains* Froude detailed his youthful battles with sin and temptation and his growing awareness of spiritual discipline and mortification. This aspect of Tractarian ascetics was then carried a stage further by Pusey, whose first contribution to the Movement in 1834, *Tract* 18, was significantly on the subject of fasting. By 1837 Pusey and his wife had sold their carriage and horses, and Mrs Pusey's jewels, in order to build churches in London. But it was the deaths of his wife and daughter, and the condemnation by Oxford University in 1843 of his sermon *The Eucharist a Comfort to the Penitent*, that brought on a new depth of spiritual depression in Pusey reflected in his extraordinary letter of 1844 [Document 19]. While the modern reader might find the language and sentiments rather pathological, it must be remembered that this acute awareness of personal sinfulness has a long tradition among Christian ascetics, and in Pusey's case it was to lead him to identify with, and translate the works of, Jean Joseph Surin, the great seventeenth-century Jesuit mystic. In the opinion of John Saward, this places Pusey firmly within the tradition of the 'fools for Christ's sake', a long history of Christian protest against conforming the Gospel to the false wisdom of the secular world.[60]

In the case of many others including Pusey, it also led to the practice of confession. In the early 1830s this was something which had effectively died out in the Church of England; indeed, in his *Tract* on fasting Pusey lamented the loss of penitential discipline in the national Church which at that time 'furnish us chiefly with that which they mainly cherished, a *general* abhorrence of sin, then guide us not to trace it out in the lurking corners of our own hearts'.[61] Thus, the modern practice of confession in the Anglican Church was initiated by the Tractarians, and Pusey was very much the central figure in this, hearing his first confession in 1838, although not making his own confession to Keble until 1846. But clearly Pusey and other Tractarians had an immense problem when trying to introduce the practice of confession into a Church with no living tradition of it. This largely obliged him to turn to the penitential guides and manuals used in the Roman Catholic Church mainly dating from the Counter-Reformation period of the sixteenth and seventeenth centuries. By the mid-1840s he had begun the process of translating these works into English.[62] Then in 1846 in his sermon *The Entire Absolution of the Penitent* he effectively advocated repeated or habitual confession, as he discovered that many of his penitents sought this.[63] And he also became the founder of the first religious community of Sisters in the Church of England since the Reformation, partly in order to satisfy a growing desire for a life of penitence and service.[64] In all of these Pusey faced difficulties and opposition. In 1850, for example, Bishop Samuel Wilberforce prevented Pusey from hearing confessions in his Oxford diocese as he objected to the habitual nature of Pusey's practice; Pusey was able to continue to do so in his college, Christ Church, as that was outside the jurisdiction of the bishop. The older High Churchmen, while affirming the ability of the priest to pronounce absolution, saw this in terms of the public liturgy not the private confessional, and also disliked the Roman manuals and the habitual element in Pusey's practice.[65] For Anglican Evangelicals and Dissenters only God could forgive sins, and the intervention of a priestly intermediary again smacked of the Romeward tendencies of the Oxford Movement.[66]

While many of their fellow churchmen saw in Pusey or Froude the same proclivity to 'enthusiasm' previously criticized as typical of early Methodism, the Tractarians themselves saw their desire for holiness in very different terms.[67] One thing they criticized the Evangelicals for was their subjective emotionalism. The Tractarians believed that the intuitive and imaginative responses evoked, for instance, by Romanticism needed to be disciplined and channelled by the Church, a view that clearly lay behind Keble's *Christian Year* in 1827. Indeed, it was Keble's personal example that many of the early Tractarians like Froude or Isaac Williams saw as their first encounter with true holiness. For both of these young men it was the reading party in the Long Vacation of 1823 under Keble's tutorship that was to have such a profound influence on their spiritual development.[68] As Williams noted: 'to find a person always endeavouring to do one good, as it were, unknown to one's self, and in secret, and even avoiding that his kindness should be felt and acknowledged as such, this opened upon me quite a new world.'[69] Keble's holiness was characterized by its undemonstrative and hidden nature; he came to personify what Tractarians called 'Reserve'. And here was a link with the High Churchmen and the Hackney Phalanx who had criticized the Evangelical Bible Society for propagating Holy Scripture among the unlearned without any comment or guidance.[70] In effect, the Tractarians took over this High Church tradition and made it their own. It was in his two *Tracts*, number 80 in 1838 and number 87 in 1840, that Isaac Williams formalized the concept of Reserve. As with so much else in the Oxford Movement, this found its starting point in antiquity, as Williams argued: 'First of all, as our Lord in the flesh concealed His divinity and His miracles, so did the *disciplina arcani* of the early Church do the same.'[71] The *disciplina arcani* was the practice of the early Church of holding back, or reserving, the most sacred parts of Christian doctrine from pagans or catechumens until they had demonstrated that they were spiritually and morally ready to receive them. Williams contrasted that with the modern Evangelical practice of 'unreserved discourse on the holiest subjects'.[72] This Williams saw as nothing more than 'a method of human desire' which ran counter to both the words of Scripture and the practice of tradition.[73] In contrast to that, Williams insisted that

> Religious doctrines and articles of faith can only be received according to certain dispositions of the heart; these dispositions can only be formed by a repetition of certain actions. And therefore a certain course of action can alone dispose us to receive certain doctrines; and hence it is evident that these doctrines are in vain preached, unless these actions are at the same time practised and insisted on as most essential.

Of these actions he noted that 'charitable works will alone make a man charitable', and 'he only will be humble in heart who does humble actions', and 'good works consist especially in Prayers'.[74] This was not the method or teaching of the Anglican Evangelicals or Dissenters, and Williams was harsh in his criticisms of them [Document 20]. Not surprisingly the Evangelicals objected strongly to the Tractarian interpretation of Reserve, arguing that it contradicted some of the words of Jesus, tended only to be employed in times of persecution by the early Church, and that its practitioners in antiquity had learnt it from the pagans.[75] Yet again these two Movements diverged in their interpretations of the Christian message.

Conclusion

Thus Tractarianism as a belief system emerges as a dynamic rather than a static phenomenon. It changed and evolved over time, and different individual leaders came to personify different aspects of it. It is therefore as difficult to give a fixed definition of Tractarianism as it is to define Puritanism in an earlier age.[76] Both are equally as slippery as the proverbial bar of soap. A Tractarian in 1845 could be rather different to his predecessor only a decade earlier, and neither would be quite the same as their successors in 1875. Not only that, at any given time different individuals or groups within the Movement could emphasize different aspects of it; some still retained much of the feeling and character of the older High Churchmen, while others would be far nearer to Rome in thought and practice. The Tractarians themselves were probably wise in refraining from any formal self-definition. However, in attempting to distinguish themselves from other churchmen they came to adopt in their personal correspondence the Greek word *ethos* to describe their Movement. *Ethos* means the character or spirit of a person, community or system; the nature or disposition of the phenomenon so described is different from others. Tractarianism, as it evolved over time, certainly had a different ethos as was increasingly perceived by other churchmen. In a host of beliefs and attitudes the Oxford Movement represented a fundamental break with the Anglican past. But when did that break begin?

3

Events

The Oxford Movement was born during the years of crisis in the relationship between the Church of England and the State from 1828 to 1833. In many ways the continuing history of the Movement was also one of a series of crises, mainly played out within the setting of the university, but with increasingly wider implications. However, as time passed, it became clear that this was far more than just a reaction by a handful of clerical Oxford dons to a particular set of events; their campaign represented a far-reaching programme not only to change the basis of the relationship between the Church and the State but also to change the very nature of the National Church itself. This would involve the effective abandonment of one historical authority, the Reformation, and its wholesale replacement by antiquity, with all that that implied for the beliefs and practices of the Church. Not surprisingly, as the implications of this began to be realized, these new Tractarians faced growing opposition both within the university and beyond, and their campaign expanded from being a largely academic venture into one of national significance. But before we can begin to trace these developments we must start with a discussion of when it all began and what to call it.

Dates and names

As we have seen, the traditional starting point for the Oxford Movement was the year 1833, and more specifically Sunday 14 July, the day Keble preached his Assize Sermon. This was the date accepted by the 'classic' accounts such as Newman's *Apologia* or R. W. Church in his history. Modern scholars, however, are far less certain of the significance of this particular date. As early as 1933 F. L. Cross in his biography of Newman added an Appendix to his book entitled 'the Myth of July 14' where he made it clear that not all the early supporters of the Movement shared Newman's reverence for that day.[1] In his 1958 biography of Newman, Louis Bouyer again raised doubts over the uncritical acceptance of that particular Sunday, although he could not offer a better alternative.[2] More recently scholars have suggested some potential alternatives to this day in 1833. Peter Nockles, for instance, sees the year 1829 as a better candidate, as that was the time of Catholic Emancipation, and specifically of Robert Peel's failure to be re-elected as a Member of Parliament for Oxford University. Peel had previously opposed Catholic Emancipation and his change of mind in 1829, he believed, obliged him to stand down and seek re-election by the university. The successful campaign against him was, at least in part, organized by Newman and his friends and was the first occasion in which they combined in an issue of national significance. Nockles therefore argues that 1829 'deserves to be regarded as an even more appropriate date for the rise of the movement' than 14 July 1833.[3] Piers Brendon, in his biography of Froude, certainly agrees that the genesis of the Movement pre-dates 1833, although he is reluctant to be so precise in selecting an alternative date as Nockles. He sees the period 1828–30 as crucial, as these were the years in which Newman and Froude were brought into closer co-operation by the political changes then under way, but argues that the crucial event was not Peel's failure to be re-elected, but the more narrowly academic battle over the role of tutors within Oriel College. This was a campaign waged by Newman, Froude and Robert Wilberforce to reform the tutorial system in a way more in tune with their spiritual, pastoral and academic ideas, and as such it 'cleared the path' for the Oxford Movement in Brendon's opinion. For him this was the 'Tractarian overture' in which many of the main themes of the Movement first appeared, from the emphasis on religious truth, to the revolutionary nature of its vigorous campaigning.[4] Stephen Thomas also agrees that the late 1820s were the crucial years, and argues that 1828 marked the start of a transition for Newman between Evangelicalism 'and a new party he was to create for himself'.[5] Thus, many of the most recent scholarly works on the Movement no

longer accept 1833 uncritically as its starting point, but all see the
origins of the Movement in the five years or so before Keble's
Assize Sermon. There are parallels here with the modern reluctance
to accept traditional starting points for other great movements,
religious or otherwise. Luther's issuing of his Ninety-Five Theses in
1517 has traditionally been seen as the starting point of the
Reformation, although few modern historians would ascribe quite
the significance to it as their predecessors. In the same way it is now
much more difficult to accept Keble's sermon as other than an
important event, but probably not the exact moment at which the
Oxford Movement began. In the absence of a generally accepted
alternative perhaps the best we can now say is that the phenomenon
we call the Oxford Movement had its origins in the crisis years of
1828–33 and that the Assize Sermon represents more a stage in the
process of genesis than it does the precise moment of birth.

The next question is what to call this Movement. Today it is
accepted that the name most often employed is 'Oxford Movement'
and its adherents are 'Tractarians'. It took rather a long time for
these to emerge as the generally accepted terms. Clearly, they derive
from the fact that the Movement began in Oxford University and
its most typical published expression was the *Tracts for the Times*.
However, like the words 'Puritan', 'Quaker' or 'Methodist', these
were names normally first coined as nicknames often by the
Movement's critics. The first recorded use of the word 'Tractarian'
did not in fact occur until 1839 in a sermon by Christopher Benson,
the Master of the Temple in London.[6] But it was far from universally accepted and other nicknames derived from the *Tracts* were
also current in the 1830s and 1840s, some of them apparently
invented by Richard Whately, the Anglican Archbishop of Dublin.
Among these were 'Tractite', 'Tractator' and 'Tractist'.[7] Certainly
Whately himself was still using the term 'Tractite party' in a letter of
1846, and the Evangelical, William Goode, called them 'Tractators'
in 1842.[8] But these were not the only nicknames used in the early
years of the Movement. During the 1840s words such as 'Oxford-
ism' and 'Puseyite' were also in vogue, the latter becoming common
after Newman's conversion in 1845.[9] Some were derived not only
from Pusey but also Newman, such as 'Newmanites', or 'New-
maniacs' or 'Newmanians'.[10] However, by about 1850 there is
evidence to suggest that the word 'Tractarian' had become fairly
widely recognized throughout the country as the nickname by
which the Movement's supporters were generally known. In 1852,
for instance, Henry Newland, the incumbent of Westbourne, tra-

velled to Brighton to deliver three public lectures and in them described himself as a Tractarian and used the word freely and fairly exclusively in his orations, without any need to explain further to his audience its derivation or application. The assumption was that they knew what the word meant.[11] The term 'Oxford Movement' was also in use at the time, at least from 1841, but as late as the 1880s was still being put in inverted commas.[12] And to confuse matters still further, among themselves the early Tractarians invented their own nicknames or code words; they referred to themselves as 'Apostolicals', the old High Churchmen as 'Z's', and the Evangelicals as 'Peculiars', because of their peculiar or distinctive theology. Yet another term that is now widely applied to all types of High Churchmen is 'Anglo-Catholic'. This, along with 'Anglican', was a seventeenth-century invention, and originally meant to apply to all those who belonged to the Established Church. The Tractarians themselves used the title *Library of Anglo-Catholic Theology* for their edition of the works of the seventeenth-century Divines. Gradually the Tractarians came to appropriate this label to their party exclusively rather than to the Church of England generally, and thus it acquired its modern meaning.[13] Then from the late nineteenth century the Movement began to be called the 'Catholic Revival'.[14] This expression is still quite frequently used to describe it.[15] It is, perhaps, a rather unsatisfactory description as it would seem to imply either that something resembling the Movement's concept of Catholicity had been previously existing within Anglicanism, which is open to debate, or that the continuous High Church tradition before the 1830s was not in any sense 'Catholic', which its supporters would have resented. Thus we have inherited from the nineteenth century a variety of possible names for the particular set of beliefs and practices that Newman and his friends initiated at the University of Oxford. This lack of clarity and precision in naming the Movement probably reflects the lack of a clear initial statement of its aims or beliefs discussed earlier. And these problems of dating and naming the Movement extend further into the difficulties of delineating its membership.

Routes to Tractarianism

It was no accident that Tractarianism had its origins in the University of Oxford. In the early nineteenth century Oxford and Cambridge were the only universities in England, and they were both exclusively Anglican institutions. All undergraduates had to subscribe to the Thirty-Nine Articles of Religion of 1563, the essential body of belief for the Church of England, which effectively excluded Dissenters and Roman Catholics. They then followed a course of study based upon Classics, Mathematics and Divinity. In addition the Fellows who constituted the governing bodies of the colleges which made up the universities had normally to be both in holy orders and unmarried, a surviving vestige of their medieval monastic origins. And at a time when no theological colleges existed, the two universities educated the overwhelming majority of the Anglican clergy from archbishops to humble curates. Each year more than half of the new graduates proceeded to ordination in the Established Church. The two universities were thus essential elements in the make-up of the Church and State, educating not only future Prime Ministers and Cabinets, but also the bench of bishops; if London was the political heart of the Establishment, then the universities were its ecclesiastical lungs breathing spiritual life into the body politic. And of the two, it was Oxford that acquired a reputation for greater adherence to orthodoxy; Oxford had been at the centre of Laud's High Church reforms under Charles I, while Cambridge had become much more the home of Evangelicalism. By the 1820s the Evangelicals had still not gained more than a toehold in Oxford, only one of its colleges, St Edmund Hall, being notable as an Evangelical centre.

In the early nineteenth century it was Oriel that was the predominantly intellectual college within Oxford University, and it was to this college that most of the original leaders of Tractarianism eventually found their way. Under its brilliant Provost, Edward Copleston, who held this office from 1814 to 1828, Oriel attained an eminence in the academic world unrivalled in its day. This was partly based on the Fellows that Copleston attracted to the college, and the unique system of examination that was employed to select them, minds remarkable not so much for the extent of their knowledge as for the way in which they employed their learning. These so-called 'Noetics', from the Greek for things pertaining to the intellect, were to play a crucial role in the preparatory phase of Tractarianism, but the very liberalism of their thinking was later to bring them into bitter conflict with Newman, Froude and other early leaders of the Movement.

The first and most senior in age of these future Tractarians to arrive at Oriel was John Keble. Born in 1792 at Fairford in Gloucestershire, the son of a High Church clergyman, it was from the countryside of that county that he first developed his profound love for the mysteries of nature. In 1806 at the age of 14 he became an undergraduate at Corpus Christi College, and having attained the extraordinary distinction of a Double First Class Degree, in 1811 at the age of 19 he was elected to the coveted Fellowship of Oriel College. Ordination followed in 1815, and the academic and ecclesiastical worlds seemed to lie at his feet; a brilliant career leading to the highest offices in the land now stretched before him. What was so amazing about Keble, and so awe-inspiring to those who knew him, was his deliberate turning aside from this path. He was for many the living embodiment of those Tractarian virtues of Reserve and holiness. From 1817 to 1823 Keble was a tutor at Oriel, renowned not so much for his academic abilities as for the strong pastoral sense he brought to his duties, something which he passed on to some of his pupils and colleagues. The infirmity of his father led him to retire from Oxford in 1823 to serve in the humble role of curate assisting his father's parish. Yet he continued his association with the university mainly through the reading parties he held in the Long Vacations for undergraduates preparing for ordination. This relative obscurity was transformed in 1827 when he published *The Christian Year*; typically Keble himself had been reluctant to publish this collection of poems that he had been writing over the previous years, and it was only the consistent pressure of his friends that finally persuaded him. He now found himself one of the most widely read poets of the age, and in 1831 his university elected him to the Professorship of Poetry, an office he was to hold for only four years, but during which he delivered some of the most influential lectures on poetry of the century. In 1835 he finally married, and in the following year he became Vicar of the small Hampshire village of Hursley, where he was to remain until his death in 1866.

Richard Hurrell Froude was born in 1803, like Keble into a traditional High Church clerical family, his father being Rector of Dartington and Archdeacon of Totnes in Devon. Also like Keble, Froude was heavily influenced by Romanticism, which in his case led to a love of the sea and sailing, a passion for medieval Gothic architecture, combined with a melancholy nature that drew him to experiment with ascetic practices. In 1821 he went up to Oriel College as an undergraduate, and in the summer of 1823 joined Robert Wilberforce and Isaac Williams in one of Keble's reading parties, almost a school of future Tractarianism. There is little doubt that Keble was one of the greatest influences on Froude's life, especially in his Reserve and holiness; in meeting Keble, Froude increasingly believed that he had come the nearest he ever would to encountering a living embodiment of that sanctity he so admired in the early Church and in the Middle Ages. In 1826 Froude too was elected a Fellow of Oriel, and in the following year became a tutor with rooms above Newman's. In the years that followed, Newman grew from his Evangelicalism in directions that brought him more and more into sympathetic contact with Froude, a friendship cemented in the battle over the role of tutors within Oriel. It was also from 1825–6 that Froude began to acquire his more obviously Catholic views, reading the Fathers and, like Newman, believing that he had a vocation to life-long celibacy. There is little doubt that in the late 1820s and early 1830s Froude was very much in the vanguard of emerging Tractarianism, a comet that shot its way across the ecclesiastical firmament drawing others in his fiery tail. Or, to use the metaphor that Froude himself employed when describing his relationship with Keble, Keble was the fire but Froude was the poker which stirred his embers to flame.[16] And Froude saw the one good deed in his life as having 'brought Newman and Keble to understand each other'; in the 1828–33 crisis these three men were at the heart of the campaigns which emanated from the university. As Piers Brendon has argued, if Keble was the saint of Tractarianism, and Newman its eventual leader, then in its initial stages Froude was the supreme agitator.[17] However, his growing symptoms of consumption forced him to leave England in November 1833, and to try to recover his health in Barbados, from whence he kept in touch with the burgeoning Movement by letter. In May 1835 he returned to Oxford for the last time, and from there home to Dartington for the final months of his short life, still writing to encourage his friends in their great endeavours, until his death in February 1836.

John Henry Newman, born in 1801, was, in the opinion of one of his most recent biographers, 'the greatest of English theologians'.[18] He eventually became not only the leader of the Oxford Movement but also a thinker whose influence has extended way beyond both England and the nineteenth century. This has led some writers to adopt an almost reverential attitude to his life and work, and consequent lack of critical content, perhaps the major fault of the two-volume biography by Meriol Trevor published in 1962, almost the last gasp of the 'great man as hero' historical tradition in Oxford Movement studies.[19] But, as we shall see later in this chapter, Newman is not beyond criticism. Unlike Keble and

Froude, however, Newman did not come from a clerical background, his father having been a partner in a small bank that failed in the aftermath of the victory at Waterloo and subsequent economic depression. It was at that time, in 1816, that Newman experienced his first religious conversion, to Evangelicalism, and his arrival as an undergraduate at Trinity College, Oxford. Recognized as one of the most intellectually gifted young men of his generation, he at first disgraced himself by failing to attain anything other than the most basic of passes in his degree in 1820. He redeemed himself in the examinations for the Oriel Fellowship to which he was elected in 1822. It was the Noetics of Oriel who first challenged his Evangelicalism, Edward Hawkins arguing that the Bible was never intended to teach doctrine but rather existed to prove it, William James who first introduced him to the concept of the Apostolic Succession during a walk in Christ Church meadow, and above all Richard Whately who taught him how to think for himself in a logical way.[20] He was ordained deacon in 1824, and priest in 1825, and his first experience of parochial work in the parish of St Clement in Oxford made him rethink some of his Calvinist views about humanity divided into the elect and the damned. But this shift away from Evangelicalism left his intellect open to the liberal tendencies of the Noetics, and in the mid-1820s that was the direction he seemed to be moving in. But the death of his sister, Mary, in January 1828 affected him deeply; intellectual brilliance was fleeting in the face of human mortality. That summer he began his systematic study of the Fathers, and then joined with Froude and Robert Wilberforce in the campaign to reform the tutorial system. That, and his opposition to Peel's re-election in 1829, brought him into conflict for the first time with the Noetics and the new Provost of Oriel, Edward Hawkins. By 1830 the three tutors had had their pupils removed from them, and Newman finally closed his Evangelical phase by resigning his membership of their various societies. But a new field was opening for him as in March, 1828 he had become Vicar of the University Church, St Mary's, and it was from that pulpit that he was to preach most of his great Anglican sermons. Newman became one of the greatest preachers in the history of English Christianity, and it was undoubtedly the attractiveness of his style, along with that of Keble, after the growing formalism and aridity of Evangelical sermons, that brought so many of that party over to the Tractarian cause.[21] The originality, drama and eloquence of Newman in the pulpit were witnessed by many in the 1830s and James Anthony Froude,

Richard Hurrell's younger brother, has left a short account of the impact Newman could have on his hearers [Document 21].

The fourth and final originator of the Oxford Movement was Edward Bouverie Pusey. Born in 1800, the second son of a relatively minor landed family, he went up to Christ Church, Oxford, as an undergraduate in 1819. Following a Double First he was elected to a Fellowship of Oriel College in 1823 and met Newman for the first time. However, Pusey was never part of that original 'inner circle' around Newman, Keble and Froude, and from 1825 he was periodically absent from Oxford pursuing his studies in Hebrew and other Oriental languages in Germany; indeed, his first major publication in 1829 was an inquiry into the historical reasons for German rationalism. In that year he was appointed Regius Professor of Hebrew, ordained, and the following year became a Canon of Christ Church, offices he was to hold for the rest of his long life. There was no doubt that Pusey was already a man of outstanding learning based on long hours of study, but by the time the first *Tracts* were published in 1833 he was still not part of the campaign launched by that inner circle. Only in January 1834 was his first contribution to the *Tracts* published, number 18 on fasting, and then, unlike the other *Tracts* which were officially anonymous, he attached his initials to the bottom of his *Tract*, ironically not so much to draw attention to himself as to distance himself from the other contributors.[22] Pusey's academic eminence within the university, and his social connections in the world of the landed aristocracy, in Newman's words 'at once gave to us a position and a name'.[23] But at that stage Pusey was still far from being a convinced Tractarian. Rune Imberg has followed the progress of Pusey's theology through the various editions of his *Tracts*, and in the first edition of number 18 he still retained a much more positive attitude to the Reformers, calling them the 'Founders of their Church', and was much less enthusiastic about the Apostolic Succession than Newman or Froude.[24] It was not until the second half of 1835 with his three massive *Tracts* on baptism that he 'more definitely sided with the Tractarians'; even so, Imberg argues that while he criticized Reformers like Calvin and Zwingli, he still retained a much more positive attitude towards Luther.[25] Only in 1837–8 did Pusey finally alter his theological views sufficiently to be in harmony with the other Tractarians, evidenced by hundreds of hand-written changes on the text of his baptism *Tracts*, now seeing all Protestants as fundamentally the same and ceasing to call them 'churches' but rather 'bodies'.[26] By 1845 the process was complete as now all references to the Reformers had been deleted from *Tract* 18, and anti-Roman Catholic references greatly softened.[27]

So Pusey was not as much of an originator of Tractarianism as the other three, his conversion to its ideas coming some years later. At the same time much of his distinctive contribution to the Movement was in some contrast to the other leaders. Pusey took Froude's and Newman's ideas about ascetics and holiness further into the areas of penitence and human unworthiness before the majesty of God. As Imberg has remarked, from his very earliest contributions to the *Tracts* there is a change of vocabulary, Pusey speaking more of 'humiliation', 'chastening of the spirit', and 'charity'.[28] Pusey was a different personality; as early as 1833 Isaac Williams noted this difference, contrasting him with Newman: 'they had been Fellows of Oriel together and Newman was the senior. But Pusey's presence always checked his lighter and unrestrained mood; I was myself silenced by so awful a person.'[29] The death of his wife in 1839 darkened Pusey's mood even further, his sense of self-loathing in his letters, and his lengthy writings on penitence confirming this. It should come as no surprise, then, that Pusey was very much instrumental in the revival of both auricular confession and the Religious life in the Church of England. On top of that his sermons and other writings were often enormous in length, hugely detailed, and lacking in the quicksilver clarity that was a hallmark of Newman. For all these reasons Pusey often seems a far less attractive figure to the modern reader, more heavily 'Victorian' in feel than the other leaders, the only one who was not a poet. Yet however uncongenial he may be to a modern audience, he clearly touched a nerve in his own times and fed a longing experienced by many Victorians dissatisfied by the growing wealth, but increasing forgetfulness of God, that they saw in their world. As Geoffrey Rowell has remarked in relation to Pusey: 'Penitence is not punishment, it is at its heart an expression of love, a response to the greatness of the love of God, in creation, redemption and sanctification.'[30] This was what Pusey saw as lacking in his day, and sought to remedy.

Oxford battles

The crises through which Tractarianism passed came in a number of phases. The first of these extended from the late 1820s to 1833, and covered the formative years of the Movement not only in terms of some of its central ideas but also in the sense of young men 'cutting their teeth' in preparation for the larger conflicts that were to come. The first of these crises began in 1828 when Sir Robert Peel announced his conversion to the concept of Catholic Emancipation. Peel had been Chief Secretary for Ireland from 1812 to 1818 and had won a national reputation when he delivered a speech opposing Emancipation in the House of Commons in 1817 and was subsequently elected MP for Oxford University as the champion of Church Establishment.[31] However, as the 1820s progressed he became less and less convinced of this position and, not for the last time in his career, came to believe that political necessity outweighed all other considerations and publicly abandoned his previous position. His support for Emancipation, he believed, obliged him to stand down as MP for Oxford University and seek re-election. This he did in February 1829. Newman, Keble and Froude now emerged as some of his leading opponents within the university, and helped to organize the campaign in which he was defeated. For the first time these future Tractarians had combined in a successful battle for the defence of that very Establishment which only a few years later they would see as an equal threat to the liberty of the Church of England.

This victory was quickly followed by a new conflict over the role of the tutors in Oriel College. In the Lent term of 1829 Newman, Froude and Robert Wilberforce altered the college timetable in such a way that they would supervise their own pupils more extensively than the general body of undergraduates. Behind this new scheme lay the same concerns that Keble had already expressed for his pupils. These men were priests as well as academic tutors and they believed that their responsibilities to their pupils thus extended to their pastoral as well as intellectual care; they had the moral welfare and religious development of their pupils in their hands as much as the academic. Unfortunately they failed to inform the Provost, Edward Hawkins, of their changes. He was furious. For him the dangers in what his unruly young tutors were doing lay in the possibilities of favouritism for some and neglect for others among the undergraduates. The tutors responded that from a narrowly academic perspective experience showed that the Oriel men who had won the highest honours in the past were those who had paid for private tutors anyway. Finally in June 1830 Hawkins acted and cut off the supply of new pupils to the three tutors. His action in many ways marked the beginning of the end for the academic pre-eminence of Oriel; he had effectively removed the

most brilliant scholars and teachers in the college from any mean-
ingful contact with the undergraduates. Within weeks he began to
realize the consequences of his actions and attempted to negotiate a
compromise with the tutors, in the end unsuccessfully. But some of
the leading ideas of Tractarianism had had a first rehearsal, that
combination of the centrality of religion in all aspects of life, the
defence of a traditional system by radical reinvigoration, and the
deliberate shock tactics used in a determined campaign.

From 1830 the battles then resumed their political nature with the
agitation surrounding the passing of the first Reform Act in 1832.
Newman, Keble and Froude were adamant in their support of the
Anglican bishops in the House of Lords who mainly opposed
reform and suffered the consequent penalties, the Archbishop of
Canterbury being pelted by a mob in the streets and the Bishop of
Bristol having his palace burned down. This period of political
opposition culminated in July 1833 when Keble warned of the dire
consequences of the proposed suppression of the ten Irish bishoprics in his Assize Sermon. Keble's sermon was quickly followed by a
meeting in the rectory of Hugh James Rose at Hadleigh in Suffolk,
where Rose and other High Churchmen met Froude to discuss
future action. Froude was not impressed. He saw them as 'con-
servatives, too timid to envision or countenance the radical Apos-
tolical gospel which he was attempting to propagate'.[32] The older
High Churchmen came from a tradition of working within the
Establishment through societies and committees based in London.
A move away from Oxford and a loss of the dynamic element that
could only come from individuals were not to the taste of the new
Tractarians. As Newman wrote at the time: 'I am for no committee,
secretaries etc. – but merely for certain individuals in every part of
the country in correspondence with each other, instructing and
encouraging each other.'[33] The one reluctant concession the Tractarians made was to allow the High Churchmen to form an 'Association of Friends of the Church' which drew up an address signed
by 7000 clergy and presented to the Archbishop of Canterbury in
February 1834 with a similar address by 230,000 laity to the King in
May 1834. But from that point onwards the Tractarians were
increasingly a separate force leading their own campaign.

External assaults on the Anglican exclusivity of Oxford University meant that in the critical years after 1833 the Tractarians
were able to make common cause not only with more traditional
High Churchmen but also with Evangelicals. In 1834–5 the new
Tract writers joined with churchmen of other parties when a Bill

was introduced into Parliament seeking to abolish the subscription to the Thirty-Nine Articles by all those matriculating as members of the university. This would effectively allow Dissenters into the university in the same way that they had been allowed into Parliament. One subtle, but in Newman's view crucial, difference between Oxford and Cambridge was that the latter only required subscription at graduation thus theoretically allowing non-Anglicans to reside in the university and participate in its academic life in all ways except actually taking a degree. Any compromise along these lines he saw as the thin end of the wedge.[34] The campaign was, for the time being, successful, and yet again the Tractarians had taken a prominent role in a victorious battle for the religious purity of the university.

In 1836 a new challenge arrived when the Whigs appointed R. D. Hampden as Regius Professor of Divinity. Again the Tractarians were able to combine with churchmen right across the party spectrum in opposition to the appointment of a person many saw as a dangerous liberal. It was Newman, Pusey and the High Churchman, W. F. Hook, who organized a petition within the university of 76 signatures to the Archbishop of Canterbury. Both archbishops then solemnly protested to the King, in whose name the appointment was made, and the Prime Minister who headed the government that in reality was responsible. In an amazing *tour de force* Newman sat up all night to write a pamphlet of 47 printed pages entitled *Elucidations of Dr. Hampden's Theological Statements,* in which he attempted to reveal the extent of Hampden's liberalism in his writings. The central issue for Newman was the creeds, the classic statements of faith by the undivided Church; Newman saw them as of divine inspiration and authority, Hampden, he argued, merely interpreted them as historical documents of human derivation and cast in the language of their times, and thus effectively denied that doctrines such as the Trinity and Incarnation were revealed by God. Hampden certainly did not accept Newman's interpretation of his words, and later in 1847 when he was created Bishop of Hereford, his fellow bishop Samuel Wilberforce of Oxford, finally read Hampden's Bampton Lectures for himself and discovered no heresy in them![35] Yet again Newman had selected his quotations very carefully to prove his particular case. Be that as it may, a long campaign ensued to get Convocation, effectively the university's ruling body, to condemn Hampden; this was only partially successful as the most that was achieved was his suspension from the board which nominated the Select Preachers.

Until 1836–7 the Tractarians had been largely successful in a series of campaigns from Peel's re-election onwards in which they had combined with other orthodox or conservative churchmen in efforts to preserve the theological purity of the university. As Peter Toon has noted, these common causes effectively restrained the Evangelicals from making forthright public protestations against the novel theology of the Tractarians.[36] In a similar way traditional High Churchmen had still not come to realize fully the gulf that was opening up between themselves and the younger *Tract* writers.[37] In these crucial early years of the Movement, therefore, the Tractarians were effectively given a breathing space, time in which to start influencing the clergy and laity beyond the confines of the university, and to build a network of supporters influenced by the *Tracts* and other writings. All that was to change in 1838.

Froude's death early in 1836 had been the first personal loss the nascent Movement had suffered. It is clear that he had played a crucial role in its gestation and first manifestations, if in no other way than through his immense influence over Keble, and especially Newman. Gradually, as his two friends received and read the manuscripts of his journals and diaries sent to them by his father, looked through his letters to them, and his various works of theology and history, a scheme emerged to publish some of these writings. The first part of the *Remains* appeared in 1838. It is now difficult for the modern reader to appreciate just how explosive this material was in its own day. A clergyman of the Established Church who reviled the Reformers in robust language, praised medieval saints like Becket, and used the Roman breviary in his devotions, was a concept almost obscene to the vast majority of Protestant Englishmen in the early nineteenth century. After its publication any further alliance with the Evangelicals was impossible as they reeled in horror from the revelations of popery, as they saw it, at the heart of Tractarianism. The reaction of traditional High Churchmen was scarcely less one of shock. With the *Remains* Newman and Keble seemed to have deliberately set out to offend in the deepest way possible the two most numerous and influential parties in the Church of England. Why did they do it?

Part of the *ethos* of Tractarianism was its aggression and provocation, to attack as the best form of defence, to shock deliberately, so to polarize issues that people would be forced to take sides. This had been manifested in the very vocabulary of the *Tracts*: '*choose* your side', and 'on *what* are we to rest our authority?' Newman had demanded of his clerical readers in the first of the

58

series. This was now carried a stage further with the publication of the *Remains*. Modern scholars are sure that Keble, and especially Newman, knew exactly what they were doing when they edited Froude's writings for publication. As Piers Brendon has commented: 'they had a very shrewd idea of the kind of impact the book would make', and accepted it as 'Froude represented the true, uncompromising spirit of the Movement and because they believed that wide unacceptability was the best guarantee of truth'; had not Athanasius stood almost alone against the world too?[38] But more than that it 'jolted the Movement forward in the direction in which Newman and Keble wanted it to go'; alienation of weaker souls would be more than compensated for by the renewed dedication of their true supporters.[39] Peter Nockles agrees that Newman knew exactly what he was doing in publishing the *Remains*:

> He was quite prepared to alienate the large 'orthodox body' of the Church of England whose early support had proved the Movement's life blood, if the Movement's hold over the rising generation at Oxford could thereby be assured ... the mixture of romantic historicism, youthful zest and ascetic holiness which those revelations contained, would exert an almost hypnotic appeal on his own younger followers.[40]

Or, as Sheridan Gilley has put it: 'he was giving orthodoxy the notoriety and excitement of a revolution and heresy, and thereby multiplying his followers'.[41]

The publication of the *Remains* marked a watershed in the history of Tractarianism. From 1838 onwards the Movement was under almost constant attack. Within weeks of their publication the Lady Margaret Professor of Divinity, Geoffrey Faussett, preached against them in Newman's own Church of St Mary, and that was quickly followed by Bishop Bagot of Oxford issuing the first, albeit mild episcopal censure of the Tractarians in his Charge. Moreover, the Evangelicals, led by Charles Golightly, prepared their own trap for the Tractarians. In order to re-affirm Oxford's loyalty to the English Reformers it was proposed to erect a memorial to Cranmer, Latimer and Ridley, the three Protestant martyrs burnt in Oxford under Queen Mary. Would the Tractarians agree to subscribe to the cost of this memorial? If they did so they would effectively disown Froude; if they did not, their loyalty to the reformed English Church would be called into question. After some initial hesitations, especially on the part of Pusey, they all refused to subscribe.

But now, whatever they thought of the English Reformers, Newman's own personal loyalty to the Church of his birth was being tested in other ways.

Newman's spiritual quest

In a famous passage in his *Apologia* Newman gave his own account of how his first doubts as to the validity of Anglicanism and his own theory of the *Via Media* surfaced. It is worth considering in some detail as modern scholarship has cast some very serious doubts over the accuracy of Newman's description [Document 22]. In this passage he first declares that all thoughts of Rome were far from his mind, and that his first unsettlement was therefore sudden and unexpected; Wiseman's article followed that first scare and the words of St Augustine quoted by Wiseman confirmed his initial disturbance. Let us look at these various statements in turn.

Rune Imberg has argued that Newman's Roman leanings did not come upon him quite so suddenly in the summer of 1839 as he described it in the *Apologia*. He has argued that Newman's whole *Via Media* theory was biased towards Rome from the start, and that he was emotionally and theologically drawn to Rome from some years before 1839.[42] Certainly from 1837 at least Imberg sees Newman softening his position, and all the changes to his two *Via Media Tracts*, numbers 38 and 41, 'point in a specific direction – that Newman was gradually changing his attitude towards Rome'; by 1841 he had deleted a whole passage listing 14 Roman 'errors'.[43] This, asserts Imberg, in itself must modify the details of Newman's account of the events of 1839; by then his *Via Media* was already in retreat.[44] Other evidence about Newman and his religious practices reinforces Imberg's conclusions from his study of the progressive editions of the *Tracts* in the years before 1839. Early in 1838, for instance, he began to use the Roman breviary for his own private devotions, to fast regularly, and to hear confessions. As Sheridan Gilley has noted: 'His slow transition to a more Roman ethos had begun.'[45] In other words, there is plenty of evidence that the 'thoughts of Rome' that Newman claimed were so far from his mind in 1839 had, in fact, been continuously with him for some time.

Another modern scholar who is equally, if not more, sceptical about Newman's *Apologia* account is Stephen Thomas. He first of all points out that it is very suspicious that in this passage 'Newman does not support this splendid piece of self-dramatisation by any corroboration of letters or memoranda of the time', something which he does frequently and extensively elsewhere in the *Apologia*.[46] But there is more. Thomas has read the manuscript papers that Newman produced as a result of his researches into the Monophysites. This was a heresy originating in fifth-century Egypt that takes its name from the Greek words for 'one nature' and asserts that at the Incarnation the human nature of Christ was effectively replaced by his divine nature; the orthodox belief, affirmed by the Council of Chalcedon in 451, is that Christ has two natures, human and divine in his one person. Crucially, what Thomas has found is that in 'none of these papers do we find the *method* of placing heresy which the *Apologia* describes as originating in 1839'.[47] Nowhere does Newman actually employ the rhetorical method of the mirror in his 1839 manuscripts as described in the *Apologia*. Thomas concludes that in 1839, 'He did not cook up a new method of treating Antiquity: he merely warmed up an old one.'[48] Nowhere does Newman compare the *Via Media* with Monophysitism in his papers; his views of orthodoxy remained as static as they had been since the late 1820s.[49] However, Thomas finds an alternative explanation for Newman's unsettlement. It originated not in his own researches but in Wiseman's article criticizing the Tractarian theory of the *Via Media*. Nicholas Wiseman was from 1828 to 1840 the Rector of the English College in Rome, and one of the foremost English Roman Catholic scholars of his day, eventually becoming the first Archbishop of Westminster in 1850, and Cardinal. From a study of Newman's correspondence at the time Thomas conjectures that Newman's disquiet was 'provoked not only by his own studies of the heresy, but by Wiseman's article'.[50] Thus Thomas concludes that Newman's own account in the *Apologia* cannot be accepted as an altogether accurate record of the role of heresy in the collapse of the *Via Media*; for Newman, remembering itself had become a rhetorical activity 'caught up in the elaborate structure of self-justification'.[51]

But however they originated, from 1839 Newman's doubts about the *Via Media* and thus the validity of Anglicanism grew, to culminate six years later in his conversion to Roman Catholicism and perhaps his most original single contribution to theology, the *Essay on the Development of Christian Doctrine*. For what Wiseman had exposed was the Achilles' heel of the *Via Media* theory. The simple logical conclusion of that theory was that Anglicanism, a relatively small grouping within the totality of Christianity, was uniquely the true embodiment of that religion. It had alone found the 'golden mean' between Rome and Protestantism. This, as Wiseman implied, was the justification of all classic heresies; that the heretics were right while the bulk of the Church was wrong. Hence his quotation of St Augustine's formula '*securus judicat orbis terrarum*', 'the whole world judges securely'. As Newman realized, Antiquity was being used to judge Anglicanism, and the verdict was alarming. From 1839 onwards the history of the Oxford Movement has within it another movement, that of Newman's mind and soul. In some ways like Luther three centuries before him Newman was now personally testing the beliefs, formulas and practices of the ecclesiastical body in which he had been born; did they answer the needs of both his intellect and his spirit? Like Luther he would need time to decide, but the emerging answer was just as negative. Unfortunately for both Newman and the Oxford Movement, his growing disquiet coincided with the escalating external attacks upon the Movement following the publication of the *Remains*. For many, Newman's final decision would be the confirmation they had been seeking; were these Tractarians loyal to the English Church or really Roman Catholics at heart?

In a sense Newman's theological interest was now switching from the Apostolicity of the Church of England to its Catholicity. Having a hierarchy and priesthood which could celebrate valid sacraments was not enough; it must be a true part of that wider body of Christians of which St Augustine had written which held to the true faith. And so Newman turned his attention to that Anglican statement of beliefs, the Thirty-Nine Articles of Religion, that represented in effect the only formal definition of Anglicanism. In 1841 he published what was to be the last of the *Tracts*, number 90 'Remarks on Certain Passages in the Thirty-Nine Articles'. Here he submitted fourteen of the supposedly anti-Roman Articles to a minute survey, not only theological but also linguistic. For instance he drew a distinction between the use of the word 'Romish' in the Articles and 'Roman Catholic', between what he took to be the popular beliefs of Catholics and the formal definitions of their Church. As Sheridan Gilley has commented, such subtle distinctions could leave him 'open to the charge of sophistry'.[52] Also the fact that the formal decrees of the Roman Council of Trent were not issued until shortly after the Thirty-Nine Articles meant that any criticism of Roman doctrine in the Articles could not refer to Trent, and by implication, the contemporary beliefs of Rome, Newman argued.

Not surprisingly the publication of *Tract* 90 produced another outcry similar to the one which had followed the revelations in the *Remains*. The major difference now, however, was that while the *Remains* had elicited only a mild rebuke from the Bishop of Oxford, number 90 encountered widespread episcopal disfavour as bishop after bishop condemned the *Tract* in a series of Charges over the next two years. This left the Movement with something of a dilemma, and essentially one of its own making. One of the characteristic features of Tractarianism had been its exaltation of the episcopal office in a way and to a degree previously unseen in Anglicanism. No bishop, no Church was effectively the Tractarian motto. Now these very bishops were condemning the writers who had so extolled them, leaving the question of whom to obey, the bishops or the *Tract* writers? In continuing to follow the latter they left themselves open to the complaint neatly expressed by Whately: 'by none is a professed veneration for the episcopal office carried to a more extravagant height than by some who ... set at naught with the greatest contumely every Bishop who ventures to disagree with them'.[53] And then as the episcopal Charges began to appear, another blow fell. Frederick William IV, the King of Prussia, viewed jealously the Russian assumption of protection over the Orthodox Christians of the Near East, and the similar French position with regard to Roman Catholics. Who would protect the Protestants? In 1841 a scheme was devised in which Prussia and Britain would establish a new joint Bishop for Jerusalem to watch over the Protestant congregations. There were two fundamental problems with this for Newman and the Tractarians. First of all it would mean accepting the validity of a Lutheran Church; and second, it would intrude a rival authority against legitimate bishops. For Newman yet again the Church of England failed his test: 'Would an unambiguously Catholic Church behave in such a manner?'[54]

As Newman pondered, further blows befell the Tractarians. In 1842 there was an election for the Professorship of Poetry at Oxford and the Tractarian, Isaac Williams, seemed an ideal candidate. However, everything had become so 'politicized' in the university that anything a known Tractarian did or stood for would be opposed on purely theological grounds. Williams withdrew his candidature when he secured only 623 pledges to his rival's 921. The following year Pusey himself was suspended from preaching in the university for two years when his sermon *The Eucharist, a Comfort to the Penitent* was judged to have taught error. The Tractarians were now becoming the victims of that very tactic of university condemnation which they had sought to employ against Hampden. By this point, however, Newman had himself withdrawn from the pulpit of the University Church to the small village of Littlemore, a few miles from the city. Here, in the tiny church he had built, he preached his last Anglican sermon on 25 September 1843, a moment charged with intense emotion. This was an age when public displays of grief or joy were still acceptable; the stiff upper lip of later Victorian years had not yet arrived. The congregation, many of them Newman's friends, openly wept and sobbed; Pusey celebrated the Eucharist in tears, and Newman had to pause often to control his own emotion as he delivered his sermon entitled *The Parting of Friends*, a cry from a breaking heart.

By the early 1840s, however, some of the younger adherents of the Movement were becoming more openly supportive of Rome. For them Antiquity was no longer the final judge of truth, but rather the contemporary Church of Rome. This line of argument received its most powerful exposition in 1844 when W. G. Ward published his *Ideal of a Christian Church*, which unambiguously saw modern Rome as the ideal against which the Catholicity and holiness of the Church of England were to be gauged [Document 23]. The enemies of the Tractarians now saw their chance for a final condemnation and repudiation of the Movement by the university. On 13 February 1845 the Sheldonian Theatre was packed with some 1200 MAs who had come to vote on a series of motions. Again amid high drama the motions were put to the vote. First, to censure Ward's *Ideal*; unpalatable as it was to many, the strength of pro-Tractarian feeling still remaining within the university meant that 386 voted against the motion. When the next vote was put, to deprive Ward of his degrees, the majority was even narrower, only 58 votes separated the two sides. Finally, when the last motion was proposed, to formally censure *Tract* 90, the Proctors rose from their seats and vetoed any vote on the proposition.

But for Newman, now in semi-monastic retirement at Littlemore, these public events had less and less relevance. In March 1845 his long years of research into the early Church reached their conclusion as he began to pen what many have seen as his greatest contribution to Christian theology. In his *Essay* Newman proposes 'a hypothesis to account for a difficulty'. Given that there are so many different contemporary forms of Christianity, many mutually exclusive in their beliefs, how are we to find the true one? The answer from his *Via Media* days had been from Antiquity, the undivided early Church. This static, fixed point now gave way to a dynamic understanding of the history of the Church. Newman starts with how ideas themselves develop and change over time [Document 24]. In a similar way, he argues, Christian doctrine follows a path of development, as the self-understanding of the institution evolves over time. But how does the Church distinguish the legitimate from the heretical developments? Newman devised seven tests for this organic growth, and came to the conclusion that while some Churches could satisfy some of them, only Rome displays them all. Should that hero of Antiquity, Athanasius, find himself in nineteenth-century Oxford it would not now be in the great chapels of the colleges or the University Church that he would find his home, but in an obscure side-street where mass was being said for a still-faithful remnant [Document 25]. In October 1845 Newman finally obeyed the logic of his intellect and the yearnings of his heart and was received into the Roman Catholic Church.

1845: catastrophe or opportunity?

Perhaps more myths and misconceptions surround the events of 1845 and their aftermath than anything else in the history of the Oxford Movement. For the pro-Tractarian historians such as R. W. Church and S. L. Ollard, the departure of Newman was a tragedy largely brought about by the intransigence and persecution of the authorities in both Oxford and the Established Church at large. From his extensive researches Peter Nockles can find little or no evidence to support the charge of persecution. He points out that most of the bishops who criticized *Tract* 90 in their Charges of 1841–3 were traditional High Churchmen, as were many of the leaders of the university from Vice Chancellors downwards, men who were certainly not unfavourably inclined to the Tractarians in principle.[55] Owen Chadwick has also argued along similar lines, that R. W. Church, one of the very Proctors who stopped the vote against Newman in 1845, in effect so hero-worshipped Newman that scapegoats had to be found, and for him they were the heads of the colleges.[56] Thus the myth of the persecuted hero driven from the Church of England entered into the folklore of the Movement. The truth is that Newman made a positive choice to leave the Church of England for the Church of Rome; he came to believe that not only was Anglicanism fatally flawed, but also that Roman Catholicism was the only Christian body in which the faith of the

Apostles could be found in the contemporary world. As Peter Nockles has put it: 'The key to Newman's ultimate loss of faith in Anglicanism lay in his attempt to erect a coherent dogmatic edifice on a structure never designed to support it.'[57]

Other aspects of this 'myth of 1845' concern its actual impact on the Movement. R. W. Church used words like 'catastrophe' and 'shock' to describe it, and S. L. Ollard wrote of the 'defeat and losses' of that year.[58] This view too has entered into Tractarian mythology, with C. P. S. Clarke writing in 1932: 'the leaders who were left behind presented the spectacle of brave men rallying the scattered fragments of a defeated and broken army in the face of a triumphant foe'.[59] As late as 1966 David Newsome was still writing in a similar vein: 'Pusey, left with Keble to rally the Tractarian ranks – severely reduced and dispirited after the news of Newman's secession.'[60] Were the ranks of Tractarianism 'scattered fragments', 'severely reduced' and 'defeated' and 'dispirited' by the events of 1845? There is a lot of evidence to suggest that again this view is in fact a myth. In order to demonstrate this we must consider it from a number of perspectives.

First of all, it is, perhaps, a mistake to read the reactions of the 'inner circle' of Tractarians on to the Movement as a whole. It was suggested earlier in this study that this concentration on just a relative handful of individuals could distort our view of what by 1845 was a very extensive Movement indeed. Here is a prime example of this. Keble, Pusey and the other original members of the Movement had, by 1845, known Newman for most of their adult lives and had often developed intense relationships with him during the stress of the Movement's various battles. For Keble the news of Newman's conversion, long dreaded, came as a 'thunder-bolt' and he wrote to Newman when he heard the news of his feelings 'as if the Spring had been taken out of my year'.[61] We have already noted the emotions at Newman's final Anglican sermon in 1843. And it must be remembered that denominational change at that time was an experience so traumatic that it is now difficult to appreciate the strength of feelings involved. In his *Apologia* Newman described his years after 1841 as his Anglican 'death bed'; he was not exaggerating. After he left the Church of England he did not meet Keble and Pusey again for twenty years, and was not to revisit Oxford until Trinity, his first college, awarded him an honorary Fellowship in 1877. Conversion was a form of death, with all the pain of mourning that went with it in Victorian England.

But what was experienced by his most intimate friends was not

necessarily replicated in the Movement at large. The vast majority
of Tractarians in 1845 had had little if any personal contact with
Newman in the preceding years. There is again something of a myth
here, in an assumption that it was sitting at Newman's feet while he
preached in St Mary's that attracted most of the converts to
Tractarianism. As Clarke wrote in 1932:

> The more earnest and thoughtful part of five generations of
> undergraduates had been hearing Newman or Pusey preach, and
> all the talk about the Tracts and the Movement, besides coming
> into personal contact with one or other of their disciples, or, it
> might be, with one of the great men themselves.[62]

As a mechanism for attracting converts the evidence would suggest
that 'personal contact' played only a relatively minor role. If we
outline the biographies of some of those converts, quite different
routes into Tractarianism will emerge.

Some were undoubtedly initially brought into the Movement by
personal contact, but often not quite in the way which Clarke
assumes. Edward Monro, the Tractarian incumbent of Harrow
Weald from 1842, received his degree from Oriel in 1836, from the
very college where Newman was a Fellow. But George Rundle
Prynne, the Tractarian Vicar of St Peter's, Plymouth, from 1848,
was an undergraduate at Cambridge, however, and met Pusey first
in 1843 only after coming under the influence of an old High
Churchman in Cornwall when he served as his curate.[63] James
Skinner, active at the Tractarian church of St Barnabas, Pimlico,
from 1851, was originally a schoolmaster in the Isle of Man with a
reputation as 'a violent Oxford Tract party man' from 1839 to 1841,
and only after his subsequent ordination did he meet the Movement's leaders.[64] Richard William Randall was Manning's successor at Lavington after the latter's conversion to Rome, and was
heavily influenced by Manning's sermons rather than any personal
contact with the leaders of, or actual part in, the Movement despite
being an undergraduate at Oxford during the years immediately
before 1845.[65] Another early leader of the Movement was Charles
Marriott, Vicar of the University Church in Oxford from 1850 to
1855; it was while he was the first Principal of Chichester Theological College from 1839 that Thomas Stevens, one of his students
there, fell under the influence of Tractarianism. The Stevens family
were prominent landowners in Berkshire, and squires of Bradfield
from 1751; Thomas was the third generation to be both squire and

parson of the village from 1843.[66] William Butler, the Vicar of Wantage from 1846, has left us a massive resource for understanding how Tractarian parishes worked in the mid-Victorian years with his multi-volumed *Wantage Parish Diaries*, manuscripts running to several thousand pages. His adhesion to the Movement was, however, at second-hand to its leaders, coming through his curacy to Charles Dyson, the incumbent of Dogmersfield in Hampshire, a friend of Keble during his undergraduate years.[67]

There were, however, numerous examples of other future Tractarian priests who were influenced not so much by personal contact as by reading the vast Tractarian literature. Thomas Thellusson Carter, Vicar of Clewer from 1844, was an undergraduate at Christ Church from 1827 to 1831; he met Pusey there, Froude once, but never went to hear Newman preach at St Mary's. It was while a curate at Burnham from 1833 to 1838 that he fell under the spell of the *Tracts*.[68] Meanwhile at Cambridge John Mason Neale, one of the founders of new Sisterhoods in the Church of England, began reading the *Tracts* in 1836 immediately before going up to Trinity College; however, his Evangelical upbringing meant that his switch to the Tractarian party was initially resisted.[69] Another young clergyman feeling his way towards Tractarianism was W. J. E. Bennett, the future vicar of St Paul's, Knightsbridge, builder of St Barnabas, Pimlico, and from 1852 Vicar of Frome in Somerset. An undergraduate at Christ Church from 1823 to 1826 he also never met any of the future leaders of the Movement. At that stage he was also clear as to the Protestant nature of the Church of England, but between 1837 and 1842 his published writings demonstrate that through his own growing acquaintance with Tractarian works he was moving steadily in the direction of the Movement, by the latter year 'an open and professed advocate' of it.[70] There were also old High Churchmen whose party loyalties were affected or modified significantly by Tractarianism. One of these was George Anthony Denison, Vicar of East Brent from 1845 and Archdeacon of Taunton. Although he claimed that the *Tracts* were not responsible for his lifelong position as an ' "extreme" High Churchman', his parish work at East Brent and his forthright advocacy of unmistakably Tractarian Eucharistic doctrine in the 1850s demonstrate the degree to which he was in their debt.[71] Henry Newland, the Vicar of Westbourne, was another High Churchman who was quite open in calling himself a Tractarian, and yet claimed that he owed nothing doctrinally to the Movement. It was in his early days as a parish priest that a journey to Switzerland convinced him that the laxity in the practice of their religion that he observed among the Protestants there was too much like his own parish in England, and this was why he turned to Tractarianism for inspiration.[72] Another High Churchman who shifted towards Tractarianism was William Gresley, in the 1830s attached to parishes in Lichfield and a frequent correspondent of the old High Churchmen, Archdeacon Churton and Joshua Watson; their manuscript letters in Pusey House, Oxford, detail Gresley's slow progress towards the newer Movement. In his day a popular religious novelist, by 1843 his novel *Bernard Leslie; or a Tale of the Last Ten Years* became a vehicle for showing how effective Tractarianism was in practice, and for praising its achievements.[73] But all of this was without any direct influence from Newman, in whose company, he noted in 1847, he had not been for more than five minutes in his whole life.[74]

These short biographical sketches paint a picture very much at variance from the simple mechanism described by Clarke; personal routes to Tractarianism were extremely varied and very few relied on contact with the Movement's leaders. The point here is that none of the priests described had the same emotional response to Newman's conversion in 1845 as Keble or Pusey; they were neither as intimate with him nor felt themselves to be as dependent on him as the two leaders. Thus to interpret the response of the whole Movement to Newman's departure through the letters and other writings of a handful of his closest friends is to totally distort its meaning for the larger Movement.

This interpretation is given further strength if we turn from biography to statistics. As part of my own researches into post-1845 Tractarianism I constructed a table of nearly 1000 Tractarian clergy active between 1840 and 1870.[75] While this does not claim to be a complete collection of all Tractarians, it is a large enough sample to legitimately extract some interesting trends. Figure 3.1 clearly demonstrates that at no point in the history of the Movement from the mid-1830s did Oxford University have anything like a monopoly in the production of Tractarian clergy. The consequence of this is that clearly that significant minority who graduated from other universities almost certainly did not hear Newman preach, or have any personal contact with the leaders of the Movement. Combining that with the biographical evidence indicates that Clarke and others who have followed him have made far too simplistic assumptions about the ways in which the Movement acquired its adherents.

The other part of the 'myth of 1845' concerns the impact of Newman's conversion on the size and growth of the Movement;

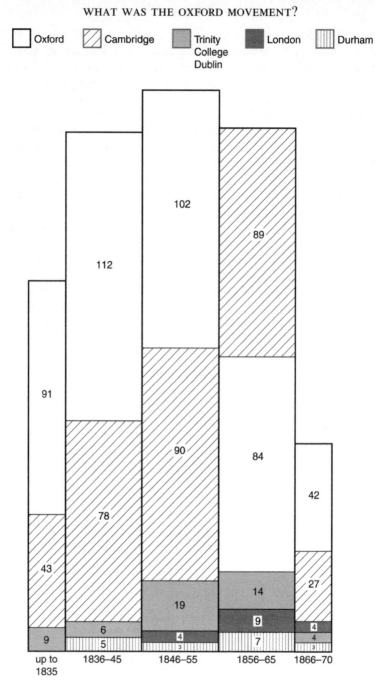

Figure 3.1 Tractarian university graduates

'scattered fragments', 'severely reduced' in size were, it seems all that were left. Again, the statistics have a different story to tell. Figure 3.2 shows the numbers of clergy leaving the Established Church for Rome in five-yearly groups. What is notable at first sight is that the largest exodus did not come in the wake of Newman's conversion, 1845–9 showing 40 conversions, while 1850–4 had 56. Thus the so-called 'Gorham Judgement' of 1850 had a much bigger impact. Bishop Phillpotts, the old High Church Bishop of Exeter, prosecuted one of his clergy, G. C. Gorham, an Evangelical, for not teaching the doctrine of baptismal regeneration, that the point of entry into the Church is at the moment of baptism, a view certainly shared by the Tractarians. Although the Court of Arches, the Church's court, upheld Phillpotts' view, the Judicial Committee of the Privy Council subsequently overturned it. Here was a secular court upholding heresy, and as a result there was a further haemorrhage of clergy from Tractarianism to Rome.

What impact did these conversions have on the actual size of the Movement? If they were as devastating as the myth assumes, then the total number of Tractarian clergy should have *fallen* in the wake of each blow. In reality, the number of incumbents actually *increased* in the aftermaths of these events, as these figures demonstrate:

1845	141 incumbents
1846	144 incumbents
1847	153 incumbents
1850	193 incumbents
1851	203 incumbents
1852	211 incumbents

The main losses on both occasions were from the ranks of the assistant curates, not the rectors and vicars, thus arguably limiting the potential damage to the Movement. In addition, Figure 3.3 and Figure 3.4 reinforce this view. Again, the statistical evidence shows a Movement steadily increasing in size. The average numbers of annual ordinations of new Tractarian clergy were as follows:

1836 to 1845	15.0
1846 to 1855	21.5
1856 to 1865	21.2
1866 to 1870	24.8

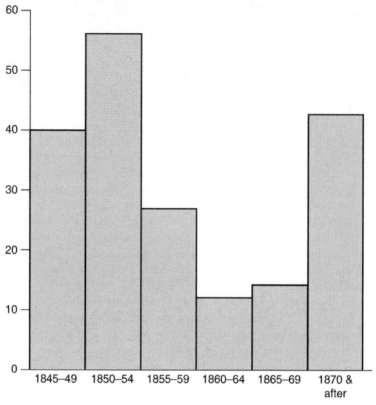

Figure 3.2 Tractarian converts to Roman Catholicism

And the total number of Tractarian incumbents rose from 81 in 1840 to 442 by 1870, an expansion of about five and a half times in 30 years.

The final element in the 'myth of 1845' was that the Tractarians were left feeling 'defeated' and 'dispirited' by Newman's conversion. Again we must distinguish between the views expressed by the leaders of the Movement who knew Newman on the one hand, and the bulk of the members of it who did not. One week after Newman was received into the Roman Catholic Church a letter from Dr Pusey appeared in the journal the *English Churchman*, clearly designed to console the Tractarians for Newman's loss. Pusey saw Newman as 'not so much gone from us, as transplanted into another part of the vineyard'.[76] The evidence, however, would suggest that Pusey was in more need of consolation than many of his fellow Tractarians. In that same edition of the *English*

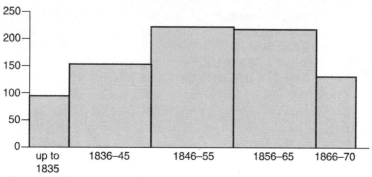

Figure 3.3 Tractarian ordinations

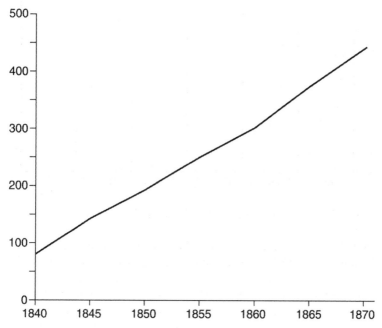

Figure 3.4 Tractarian incumbents

Churchman, but overlooked by most historians sympathetic to the Movement, was another letter from W. J. E. Bennett which took a diametrically opposed view to Pusey [Document 26]. Upon reading Pusey's letter, John Mason Neale commented bluntly, 'I cannot pretend to agree with it, because if the step was not very right, it must have been very wrong.'[77] In 1844 William Gresley had published his *Anglo-Catholicism* in which he reaffirmed a belief in the

Via Media just as Newman and the younger 'Romanizers' were about to finally abandon it. In his book Gresley explicitly criticized this Romanizing tendency for having damaged the Movement, views also shared by Bennett, Thomas Stevens, Edward Monro, T. T. Carter, George Anthony Denison and Neale.[78] When the dust from the events of 1845 had begun to settle, Gresley then published a series of essays in which he considered the effects of the Roman conversions on the Movement. It was with obvious relief that he wrote of the Romanizers: 'They are, as a party, silenced and extinguished.' In his view Tractarians were now free again to re-assert a view of Anglicanism more akin to the *Via Media* of the 1830s, to build a Church of England that would be 'in practice what she is in theory', and he looked forward to a future in which the Movement would 'make a great advance and acquire a firmer hold'.[79]

Thus, all the evidence, biographical, literary and statistical points in one direction – however traumatic the effect of Newman's loss was to Keble, Pusey and the 'inner circle', it would be a great mistake to assume that all Tractarians shared their views, or that its impact was anything like as catastrophic for the Movement as some historians have assumed. Many Tractarians greeted Newman's departure with relief, and the loss of him and the younger Roman-izers was seen rather as a great opportunity for the Movement to prove itself in the parochial world.

Conclusion

Born out of a crisis, and growing through a series of battles, the history of the Oxford Movement is undoubtedly marked by conflict and loss, and has a huge element of pathos attached to it. But we must be careful not to extend the undoubted emotions of a few of its members on to the Movement as a whole. While not minimizing the impact of the events of 1845, especially Newman's conversion, we must not see them in the apocalyptic terms that some partisan historians have done in the past. As a parochial Movement it was untouched in its steady growth. And so we must turn now from the dramas of Oxford to the relative calm of the rural world of Vic-torian England to examine the impact that the ideas of the Tract-arians were having more generally in the Church of England.

4

Parishes

Even before 1845 the Oxford Movement had acquired a life of its own, to a large degree independent of its originators in the university. They had given birth to a set of ideas that clearly answered a need among hundreds of Anglican clerics who were now carrying Tractarianism into the parishes of England. The Oriel dons had never intended that their concepts should be no more than a set of theoretical propositions to be debated and battled over in the rarefied atmosphere of dreaming spires. Their Catholic views of the Church of England were always designed to have practical consequences, nothing short of a wholesale transformation of the spiritual, liturgical and pastoral life of the Church. This aspect has too often been ignored or sidelined by historians; but to attempt to answer the question of what the Oxford Movement was without substantial reference to its practical consequences would be to see but a part of the whole picture.

Tractarian parishes

The statistical analysis of Tractarian clergy introduced in the last chapter demonstrated that between 1840 and 1870 a steadily growing number of parishes were being affected by the ideas of the Oxford Movement. But this expansion has itself to be set within a number of other contexts. First of all, it is clear that in this period Tractarians remained a numerically very small element within the Church of England. In 1841 there were 14,613 clergy in England

and Wales, and by 1871 they had increased to 20,824.[1] Against that, a figure of under 1000 Tractarian clergy identified across the whole 30-year period demonstrates how numerically weak the Movement was, in all probability accounting for under 5 per cent of the clergy even if we assume that the sample underestimates the actual number of Tractarians. But, second, what is equally clear when these figures are analysed by geographical distribution is that Tractarianism was a lot stronger in some parts of England than others. Figure 4.1 and Table 4.1 show this across the 23 dioceses of England, proving that Tractarians were at their most numerous in London, the Home Counties and the south-western peninsula. Of 612 incumbents identified in the sample, some 327, or over half, were in parishes of under 1000 souls, overwhelmingly the villages of the rural south, and another 203 were in parishes with populations of 1000 to 5000, mainly the market towns of the same region. As the Religious Census of 1851 made clear, the main strength of Anglicanism in the mid-nineteenth century was in rural areas; in going to the south of England Tractarians were merely following the trend of Anglicanism as a whole.[2] In addition, dioceses like Oxford under Samuel Wilberforce, or Exeter under Henry Phillpotts, were likely to prove sympathetic to Tractarian clergy. Finally, it must be remembered that the decades from the mid-1830s onwards saw a general revitalization in the life of the Established Church. Too often the older histories of the Movement tend to ignore this, when they mention anything at all about the parochial world, and give the impression that Tractarians were the only clergy involved in the process. In 1835 the Prime Minister, Sir Robert Peel, set up a body which the following year became a permanent one, the Ecclesiastical Commission. The reports that flowed from it led to legislation like the Established Church Act (1836), the Pluralities Act (1838) and the Dean and Chapter Act (1840), which helped to redraw diocesan boundaries, reorganized episcopal funding and cathedral finances, and started the long process of radically reducing pluralism and non-residence among the clergy.[3] For some Tractarians the problem with this approach was the involvement of the State yet again in the affairs of the Church. In 1838 Pusey lamented that 'We shall live under the supremacy of the Commission, it will be our legislative, executive, the ultimate appeal of our bishops; it will absorb our Episcopate; the Prime Minister will be our Protestant Pope.'[4] But whatever Pusey's fears, it is clear that the Commission was a vital component of Anglican revitalization in these years. And alongside that, clergy, in alliance with significant elements within the laity, were also instrumental in initiating a massive programme of reconstruction of the physical fabric of the Church of England with new schools built, and literally thousand of churches either restored or completely new ones erected. Between 1840 and 1874 it has been calculated that a sum in excess of £25 million was spent on the building or restoration of Anglican churches in England.[5] As James Obelkevitch has remarked of the period from the 1820s, 'the reconstruction of church fabrics was one of the commonest aims of reformers' of all theological persuasions.[6]

Table 4.1 Total number of Tractarian incumbents by diocese from 1840 to 1870

Diocese	No.	Diocese	No.
London	77	Worcester	26
Oxford	57	Norwich	25
Exeter	55	Carlisle	23
Rochester	44	Gloucester and Bristol	19
Lincoln	37	York	19
Bath and Wells	36	Ely	17
Chichester	34	Manchester	15
Winchester	34	Chester	14
Canterbury	31	Hereford	13
Lichfield	30	Peterborough	12
Ripon	28	Durham	6
Salisbury	26		

So what was it like to live in a Tractarian parish in these decades? One way to begin to understand how the Movement's parochial clergy viewed their parishes and parishioners is to imagine a series of concentric circles. The outermost one enclosed the whole population of the parish over whom the incumbent believed he had at least a theoretical authority, whether or not they were baptized or acknowledged any form of even the most basic Christianity. The next circle moving inwards included those whom the rector or vicar perceived as professing a flawed or corrupted type of Christianity, the Dissenters in their various sects and groupings. Merging with them, and forming the next concentric circle, were groups referred to as 'Dissenting churchmen', by which was meant those who saw no essential difference between the Church of England and other

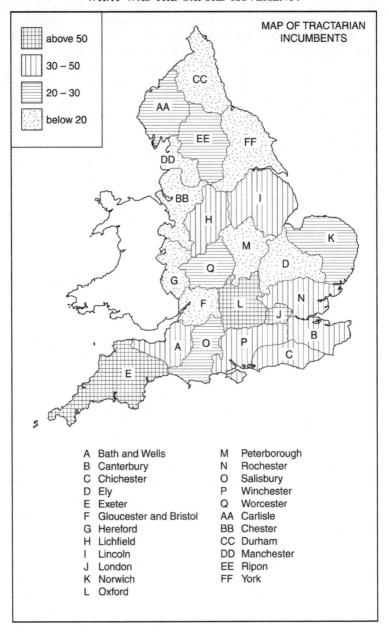

Figure 4.1 Map of Tractarian incumbents

Protestant Churches and who would, for instance, freely attend the worship of the parish church on Sunday morning and then go to a Methodist meeting house in the afternoon. A circle nearer to the centre were those who did attend worship exclusively in the parish church but were not communicants, nor had any desire to become so; they formed the backbone of the regular congregation at the so-called Daily Service. The next circle contained those preparing for Confirmation or First Communion, often the youth of the parish being prepared to join the innermost group within the final circle at the heart of the parish, the regular communicants. It was the creation of an ever-expanding Eucharistic community that the Tractarian clergy saw as the final goal of the whole parochial system, and measured their success or failure in terms of its size. All their visiting, their schools, their evening classes were part of a machine designed to produce a growing momentum from the periphery to the inner core.

Starting with the outer circles containing the Dissenters and Dissenting churchmen we shall now examine each of these groups in more detail in order to understand how a Tractarian parish worked. What is first of all quite clear is that it was these groups in the outer circles that gave the Tractarian clergy their greatest problems. All too often it was an alliance between Dissenters and the tradesmen and smaller farmers that provided the impetus for organized opposition to the work of the Tractarian clergy. Just as the originators of the Movement encountered opposition within Oxford University, so now the parochial world reproduced this, if in rather less sophisticated ways. And in the rural environment theological differences could easily merge with, or be absorbed by, economic ones; clergymen who expected shops to be closed for church festivals, who demanded an increase in the time given to church attendance, and sought a more generous attitude to the giving of alms, as the Tractarians did, were bound to come into conflict with the local representatives of Victorian commercial enterprise.

The period in which this opposition reached its peak was in the early 1850s. The year 1850 itself had witnessed two events which were to act as catalysts for this explosion of opposition. The first of these was the final act of the Gorham Judgement when the Judicial Committee of the Privy Council declared that baptismal regeneration as understood by all High Churchmen was not the sole interpretation allowed in the Church of England. The second was the so-called 'Papal Aggression' when the Roman Catholic hierarchy was restored. Of the two, it was the latter that proved to be the more serious, especially when Lord John Russell, the Prime Minister, publicly blamed the Tractarians for the Pope's actions. These years witnessed an escalation of traditional anti-Catholicism and Tractarians became targets alongside Catholics themselves.[7] W. J. E. Bennett was in no doubt that it was Russell's intervention that was responsible for the riots that began around his church of St Barnabas, Pimlico.[8] But it was not only in London that the effects were felt. At Westbourne the Tractarian vicar, Henry Newland, was also engulfed in controversy; the tranquillity of his parish was shattered when his churchwardens decided to complain formally to the Bishop of Chichester about liturgical uses that Newland had introduced without incident several years before. He had no doubts about what had prompted this, namely 'the letter of an unprincipled statesman', Lord John Russell's letter to *The Times*.[9] His biographer has left a graphic account of events in Westbourne, events that were repeated in similar ways in many other Tractarian parishes at the time [Document 27]. James Molyneux, the Perpetual Curate of St Gregory with St Peter at Sudbury in Suffolk, also recorded the lengths to which his opponents would go [Document 28]. At Wantage simmering opposition to the vicar, William Butler, finally burst into open hostility early in 1852 and centred around his plans for the restoration of the church. The local Wesleyan minister began a series of lectures on the evils of Puseyism, and the Sisters from the convent that Butler had recently founded had to go out late at night to wash the walls in the town where chalked slogans against the vicar had been scrawled during the day.[10] The climax came at the Easter vestry, Butler admitting that even he 'was not prepared for the fierce opposition I encountered'. The meeting was packed with Dissenters stimulated by the lectures of the Wesleyan minister; on the previous day handbills had appeared in the town calling upon all parishioners to go to the meeting to oppose Popery. At any mention of opposition to restoration the assembled townsfolk broke into loud cheering, and when one of the vicar's few supporters unwisely used the word 'rabble' to describe the opposition, he was almost unable to finish his speech such was the clamour. Finally, the idea of restoring the church was defeated by a large majority, Butler describing this as a 'distinct disaster'. He returned to the vicarage looking 'broken down and dejected'.[11]

This association between Dissent, opposition and particular social groups, combined with the paternalistic social attitudes that the Tractarians shared with the majority of their fellow clergy, led them to take a particular interest in their local farmers and trades-men. As David Roberts has made clear in his study of early Victorian paternalism, the theory that the social hierarchy was God-given, but that the wealthy had duties in their relations with the poor, just as the poor should show deference to the rich, was very far from being carried out in practice, and that what typifies the period was the wholesale failure of both traditional landowners and the new industrialists in their responsibilities to the poor.[12] As the nineteenth century progressed, churchmen of all parties became increasingly concerned at the social consequences of industrializa-tion, and in particular the growing separation between the classes and the failures of the wealthy to do anything to heal the growing rift.[13] Tractarian literature in these years is full of complaints about the failures of the wealthy in their role as good paternalists, W. E. Heygate, the incumbent of Sheen in Staffordshire and Tractarian novelist, expressing this bluntly: 'where the rich feast most, the poor fast most. We spend upon ourselves in things needless that would feed multitudes; and thus invert the Saviour's miracles, making bread scarce.'[14] Indeed, one of the spurs to the Tractarian drive to build and restore churches was to correct what they saw as the sin of the wealthy living in beautiful and expensive houses while the fabric of the churches was falling into decay.[15]

As the majority of the Tractarian clergy in these years were rural, it is not surprising that one of the major concerns expressed in their writings was the relationship between landowners and agricultural labourers. Tractarian novels abound with examples of charitable squires and landlords, with one favourite theme among these authors being the return of church property seized at the time of the Reformation, and so diverted from its proper use in supporting the poor.[16] Sometimes fact could begin to live up to fiction as when the Tractarian sympathizer, Earl Beauchamp, gave £60,000 to establish almshouses for elderly agricultural labourers at Newland in Wor-cestershire.[17] The Tractarian squire and parson of Bradfield in Berkshire, Thomas Stevens, bought wheat at low prices for his labourers and was always careful in his choice of tenant farmers to make sure they would pay a fair wage.[18] But all too often the local landowners and farmers were seen to be failing in their paternalistic duties, and the rural middle classes presented the Tractarian clergy with some of their most stubborn opponents: 'the farmers in this place oppose themselves to every advance, whether in matters connected with the Church or education' wrote B. J. Armstrong the Vicar of East Dereham in Norfolk after visiting a neighbouring parish.[19] W. E. Heygate turned his attention to these problems in his novel *William Blake: or, the English Farmer*, perhaps the most developed fictional treatment of rural society by a Tractarian in these years, and which he described as 'a little fruit of rural parochial work'.[20] Heygate believed 'that the farmers of England are an important class, and one hardly recognising its privileges, power and consequent responsibility', a fault he hoped to begin to correct through the writing of his novel.[21] During the course of the story William Blake is influenced by his new Tractarian rector, becomes a communicant after careful preparation, and finally emerges as the perfect model of a paternalistic farmer, reading improving literature, founding a school for his labourers (under the care and guidance of the rector), giving allotments to the poor, arranging their work so that his men could attend church, and never attempting to cheat anyone in business. But such a fictional paragon of religious and social virtues rarely materialized in fact. The pages of the *Wantage Parish Diaries* show William Butler engaged in an almost daily struggle to turn his hostile and suspicious farmers and tradesmen into good churchmen and paternalists, but with relatively little success: 'the deadness of the tradesmen and farmers to all serious matters' was still apparent to him after four years in the town.[22] Occasional success with individuals could not hide the disappointment he felt with this class. In 1855, after more than nine years of struggle in his parish, Butler was outraged that a respectable tradesman who was also one of his churchwardens had been discovered committing adultery. This produced a bitter torrent of frustration at what he saw as the failings of this class, notable for the intensity of its language [Document 29].

Moving inwards the next group in this concentric circle model of a Tractarian parish were those who attended the Daily Service. *The Book of Common Prayer* explicitly ordered Morning and Evening Prayer to be said daily by all priests and deacons and its revival in parish churches was very much associated with the Tractarians; Newman himself had instituted the Daily Service at the University Church in Oxford in June 1834.[23] In the 1840s and 1850s scores of parishes across England began to take up the practice under the inspiration of the Oxford Movement. By 1860 many rural Tractarian parishes were characterized by a full service sung to Gregorian chants by a surpliced choir twice daily, leading a regular congregation in relatively lengthy acts of worship, often including a sermon as well. Probably the most detailed evidence that has survived about the numbers and characteristics of these congregations is found in William Butler's *Wantage Parish Diaries*. Butler arrived in Wantage in 1846 and within three years was recording congregations at his Daily Service of between 27 and 60 persons. On a particularly good day, 10 July 1860, he noted 40 at the morning service and 100 at the evening, in a town of little more than 3000 people. The congregations were mostly elderly and female, among the latter Butler noting a growing number of young servant girls who rose especially early to do their work in order to be able to attend Morning Prayer.[24] Another group attracted to these relatively elaborate services were people from non-Tractarian parishes who had the money and leisure to settle for periods of time in places where the Daily Service was performed. This phenomenon, aided by the publication of special guide books, was noted by Thomas Stevens at Bradfield: 'It is quite curious that the number of applications for houses in Bradfield, because of the Church services, keeps increasing'; by 1852 he observed that he could have let 20 houses in the village to such occasional parishioners, and for the want of them the village shop had taken in lodgers for weeks at a time.[25] Bradfield was notable, however, even among Tractarian parishes for the lengths the rector would go to in order to achieve the finest choral services. Even local men and boys who applied to become his gardeners and stable lads had to have a singing test before he would employ them! In 1850 he went so far as to establish a public school in the village with the express purpose 'of supplying means for good choral services' with a choir largely composed of boys and masters.[26] No wonder that by the mid-1850s he could boast to the Dean of Carlisle that his choir was 'fully equal to those of our Cathedral choirs'.[27] By 1864 at Wantage Butler had a regular choir of 40 men and boys, even if the evidence of the *Diaries* suggests that the musical quality was no match for his near-neighbour at Bradfield.[28] Butler also had to wage quite a lengthy campaign to get his choir to wear surplices. His first tentative suggestion to this effect in 1849 was met with blank hostility, and it was not until 1857 that the choir would agree to this.[29]

All this effort to produce an elaborate Daily Service was itself but secondary to the main liturgical event in Tractarian parochial life, the celebration of the Eucharist. We have already seen how, from the earliest days of the Oxford Movement, Froude advocated the frequent celebration of the Eucharist as one of the goals of his agitation, and how the theology of the Eucharist developed in Tractarian circles in the 1840s and 1850s. Now in the parochial world the clergy influenced by the Movement began to put theory into practice, with the ideal of a celebration every Sunday and Holy Day. In the middle decades of the nineteenth century weekly Communion was exceptional in the rural parishes of the Anglican Church, and in the 1860s a weekly Eucharist 'was rare enough to be considered as a party-badge and to mark off the celebrant as a sympathiser with the Tractarians'.[30] Because such a tradition of frequent Communion had all but died out, the Tractarians were faced with enormous problems of prejudice and misunderstanding in their efforts to reintroduce it, as recorded by Edward Monro and Henry Newland [Documents 30 and 31]. Class divisions first observed in the new industrial and urban world had by the middle of the nineteenth century found their way into the countryside. Just as in the cities the new middle classes expressed their status by moving to sumptuous suburban villas clearly segregated from the overcrowded and disease-ridden slums of the poor, so now the farmers too were shifting their labourers from their traditional lodgings in the farmhouse to small cottages in the nearest village. It was but a short step from social to spiritual segregation. Elitist views of Holy Communion like those found by Monro and New-land were common, and could easily become socially divisive, engendering the widespread feeling among the poorer parishioners that partaking of Communion was not for them. On the other hand, the wealthier sections of the parish often viewed attendance at this service in particular as a badge of respectability. Thus in promoting more frequent celebrations the Tractarian clergy had a clear social as well as spiritual purpose. In the words of William Gresley:

We are accustomed to think that the Communion is intended only for certain respectable persons in the parish. Those who are well to do in the world are rather expected to come ... We forget that the exhortation is addressed to all. The table is spread for all.[31]

So how successful were the Tractarians in creating Eucharistic communities at the heart of their parishes? When W. J. E. Bennett moved to Frome in Somerset in 1852 it was a town of 12,000 people, but with only one quarter of them within the jurisdiction of his parish. During the course of his first year there Bennett increased the number of regular communicants from 620 to 710, although how many were strictly from his parish is impossible to say.[32] At the other end of the demographic scale was R. W. Ran-dall's parish containing the village of Lavington with fewer than

900 souls. On his first Sunday there he administered Communion to just 17 persons; by Christmas, 1860, this had risen to 140, or about 15 per cent of his parishioners.[33] Bradfield had about 1000 inhabitants and in October 1866 Thomas Stevens calculated that he had 95 regular communicants, or fractionally under 10 per cent of the village.[34] When B. J. Armstrong arrived in East Dereham in Norfolk in 1850 he estimated the population of the town as 4000 persons, and with 170 regular communicants. By 1865 he had only managed to increase this to 200 and was acutely aware that having only 5 per cent of his parishioners as communicants was unsatisfactory.[35] Once again William Butler's *Wantage Parish Diaries* provide a wealth of evidence on numbers, composition and methods of creating a Eucharistic community. At Easter 1848 he had some 91 communicants; by 1851 this had increased to 240, peaking at 345 in 1858. Between 1860 and 1865 the numbers fluctuated slightly between 311 and 339. Butler was dissatisfied with this plateau of about 10 per cent of his parishioners and at the end of 1867 set himself the goal of a Eucharistic community of 400.[36]

Tractarians and the parochial world

Were these rural Tractarian parishes radically different from the majority in the mid-nineteenth century? There are a number of areas where the work of the Tractarians is surprisingly similar to that of their clerical brethren; where differences do exist they are normally of degree or emphasis. Modern research on the world of the rural parishes is not particularly extensive, but what it does demonstrate is that the majority of the Anglican clergy of all parties, or none, were all involved in a number of campaigns to improve the spiritual, pastoral and liturgical life of the parishes. Increasing the frequency of Holy Communion and the creation of Eucharistic communities at the heart of their parishes were aims shared by large numbers of priests. In her recent study Frances Knight has found ample evidence for a widespread campaign by the clergy which 'aimed to identify the Anglican spiritual elite in the parish, and to mould them into a self-conscious eucharistic community'.[37] She has found much common ground in the practical approaches to creating these communities right across the spectrum from Tractarian to Evangelical.[38] This confirms the findings of earlier studies by Anthony Russell and James Obelkevitch which stress the importance of establishing boundaries of particular church membership through Eucharistic communities in a world of growing denominationalism.[39] What distinguished the Tractarians was their emphasis on weekly Communion in an environment where most were aiming for a monthly celebration. But, on the other hand, all clergy experienced the same frustrations as the Tractarians from the elitist views of the sacrament shared by so many of the laity.[40] And in a world where denominational identity was hardening, it was the Tractarians in particular who were emphasizing the theological differences between Church and Dissent, and not seeing it as just a matter of social distinction which was sometimes the case with other clergy.[41] As William Butler noted of Wantage Dissenters in his *Diaries*: 'they feel and know that we can have no peace with their principles'.[42]

One area where at first sight we might expect to find significant differences between the Tractarians and other clergy, the practice of confession, on closer inspection also reveals much that is similar. Undoubtedly there were a number of specific instances where the Tractarian practice of confession resulted in local hostility, one of the best documented being the bitter exchanges in print between John Mason Neale and his fellow cleric, John Scobell, after the latter's daughter made her confession to Neale and then joined his Sisterhood, much against her father's wishes. The daughter subsequently died while nursing scarlet fever patients, and Scobell accused Neale of deliberately engineering this in order to obtain her property which she had willed to the Sisters. A riot took place at her funeral and the two clergymen publicly exchanged a series of acrimonious letters that further fuelled the tension.[43] Another infamous case occurred in Brighton where the activities of the Tractarians William Gresley and Arthur Wagner resulted in their opponents forming the Brighton Protestant Defence Committee, one of the aims of which was to stop the practice of confession in the town. In 1854 this committee issued a public warning to all local residents, the colourful language of which was typical of many ultra-Protestant reactions to the revival of confession by Tractarians [Document 32].

But such cases as these, spectacularly public as they were, must be viewed as the exceptions rather than the rule. There was a world of difference between the sophisticated and well-educated penitents who went to priests such as Pusey in Christ Church, Oxford, and what was possible with rural parishioners. When Tractarians wrote about repentance and confession in practice this meant different things, depending upon the circumstances of the particular individuals concerned. In most cases, as modern research has confirmed, there 'was little practical difference between the Evangelical clergyman treating a case of conscience and a nineteenth-century Tractarian hearing a confession'.[44] In the rural world all thoughts of confessional boxes, regular times for confession, or indeed any sense of a formal rite being performed in church, must be banished from the picture. What the evidence reveals among the Tractarians is an infrequent, informal and highly flexible practice, usually carried out in a private house or the priest's study, and a clergy surprisingly reluctant to bring their comparatively simple parishioners to make anything resembling a formal confession. The problems were further compounded by the lack of practical experience in hearing confessions on the part of the clergy themselves; as John Mason Neale observed in 1852: 'We have, or we might have, the works of the great writers on conscience; but we have not the living experience, the training, the routine ... all is new to us, all is strange.'[45] This handicap led most priests to adopt a very flexible and non-standardized approach to confession, as one of the most important Tractarian works on the subject from this period acknowledged:

> The real utterance of the heart's secret guilt is the essence of the act; the circumstances under which it is made but the accidents ... it would be unreal not to regard a contrite expression of sin acknowledged in the least formal way ... as a true and acceptable confession.[46]

The first and most fundamental thing the Tractarian clergy had to do was to instil a sense of repentance into their parishioners; only when this was achieved would a few individuals be spiritually capable of taking this to a higher stage of verbalizing their sins in the presence of a priest. The most propitious times to try to do this were before Confirmation or First Communion, in sickness, or at the point of death. W. J. E. Bennett has left an account of such a deathbed scene that illustrates some of the limitations of the practice of confession inherent in the rural world [Document 33]. But what form of words did he or any other Tractarian priest use to pronounce absolution? This was yet another example of the practical difficulties faced by the clergy and the point where flexibility came into its own. Probably the formula in the Visitation Service in the Prayer Book was the most commonly used; but some priests composed their own words, or adapted those used by Roman

Catholics.[47] It is also highly significant that amid all of the mass of details about the daily life of his parish that William Butler recorded in the hundreds of pages of each volume of his *Wantage Parish Diaries*, there is but one short paragraph where he gives anything approaching a detailed description of the practice of confession in his parish. This, perhaps more than anything else, brings into relief the practical difficulties faced by Tractarians in this period in introducing confession into rural parishes, and illustrates the informality and flexibility that they were obliged to employ in this relatively rare and intensely private occurrence [Document 34].

There were, in addition, a number of areas where the Tractarians were in the vanguard, or at the cutting edge, of reform in the parochial world. One of the most important of these was the removal of pews and galleries. If the Eucharist was for growing numbers of clergy the model of social harmony, then pews were the antithesis of that. While by the 1860s the removal of pews had become a church-wide campaign reflected in such pressure groups as the Incorporated Free and Open Church Association, back in the 1840s the pioneers of this reform had been the Tractarians. It was John Mason Neale who had first launched this campaign against pews with a paper he read to the Cambridge Camden Society in November 1841 in which he claimed that the history of pews was nothing but 'the history of the intrusion of human pride, and selfishness, and indolence, into the worship of God'.[48] The following year Henry Manning, the Tractarian Archdeacon of Chichester, used similar language to attack pews in his Charge.[49] Many other Tractarian writers also emphasized the socially divisive nature of these intrusions into the house of God [Documents 35, 36 and 37]. The problem was that pews were individual seats, or whole rows of seats, which were effectively reserved for those who could afford to rent them and have them literally boxed off, and into which the poor were not permitted to enter. This replicated the class divisions of the secular world in the church itself, and for Tractarians the sin was compounded by pews being a post-Reformation innovation. If the Church was ever to succeed as a reconciler in a divided society they were clear that pews had to go, to be replaced by open and free benches. At St Barnabas, Pimlico, W. J. E. Bennett built the first London church of modern times in which no seats were rented or appropriated.[50] Meanwhile, in the countryside, Tractarians often had a long and sometimes bitter fight, occasionally lasting for years, to persuade pew-holders to surrender the sacred rights of property; but slowly they began to transform the seating arrangements in the church, something which may help to account for their relative success in attracting a few among the poor back to the worship of the Church of England.

Another thing that helped to distinguish Tractarians from the mass of mid-nineteenth-century Anglican clergymen was their deliberate emphasis on such things as caution and patience, as well as flexibility, when introducing reforms into their parishes. Because of their distinctive theology, and popular reputation as fanatical innovators, they had to be more circumspect than most clergy at that time. F. E. Paget, the Tractarian incumbent of Elford in Staffordshire, wrote a number of novels designed to warn his fellow Tractarians of the dangers of excessive enthusiasm. In *The Curate of Cumberworth* he portrayed a young priest eager to make changes in his parish for 'some things cry out so loudly for reform ... That the sooner one commences one's alterations the better.' But an older and wiser clerical friend advised him to be more patient as otherwise he could risk undoing much of the good work already accomplished over a number of years.[51] In *Milford Malvoisin* Paget developed his theme and described in some detail the kind of indiscretions that could cause problems [Document 38].

By the mid-1850s this careful and restrained approach appeared to be starting to bear fruit. In 1854 William Butler noted that 'the tone of the parish is friendly, and opposition has all but died out'.[52] In 1859 one of B. J. Armstrong's main opponents at East Dereham sent him a dinner invitation, and by 1862 he was able to remark on 'a wonderful softening of party feeling everywhere'.[53] At Lavington, R. W. Randall's opponents had so melted away that he could describe Easter 1860 as 'the most blessed' he had yet had in the parish.[54] Generally, by about 1860 Tractarians commonly felt that they had weathered a series of storms and could look forward to a future of much calmer conditions. Undoubtedly their cautious, restrained and flexible pastoral techniques were very much in contrast to the more confrontational *ethos* of Tractarianism in Oxford in the 1830s, but they believed that the different conditions of the rural parochial world demanded different approaches. They had come to see that the Church of England would not be so easily or rapidly overtaken by the Tractarian vision for it as the originators of the Movement expected; in the words of Henry Newland: 'We cannot hope in the few years of our lives, to restore the decay of centuries.'[55] However, there was a rising generation of younger Tractarians who were not so sure about the wisdom of this approach.

Ritualism

In the 1840s and 1850s most Tractarians regarded matters of ceremonial in church as of secondary importance. The teaching of basic theological concepts to rural congregations where the practice of regular Communion had collapsed generations before was of far greater urgency. As William Gresley argued: 'The English Eucharistic service regularly carried out needs no accession of ceremony' and advised clergy not even to light candles on their altars if the congregations had yet to understand this as a symbol of Christ's light in the world.[56] In 1850 Edward Monro warned clergy against 'hollow aestheticism' and explained that architecture and ornaments were 'but a chrysalis, in which the immortal soul is preparing to spread its wings into eternal day. We must not spend our time there', but rather 'reverse the order, and begin with the hearts of your people'.[57] The priority was to change hearts, not attract the eyes. The majority of Tractarians in these decades went no further than to place two candles on the altar, and some did not even light them during services, to wear a surplice and stole where most parish clergy still wore the black gown, and to turn eastwards to celebrate the Eucharist with their backs to the congregation, rather than stand at the north end of the communion table sideways to the congregation as the Prayer Book rubric directed. A very few Tractarians did take this further, especially the wearing of the chasuble. This was the traditional vestment worn by the priest celebrating the Eucharist and was derived from the paenula, or outdoor cloak, worn by the Roman aristocracy in late antiquity. It had evolved in the Middle Ages into a vestment of Gothic shape reflecting the architecture of the times, and had come to symbolize the presence of Christ and his sacrifice presented sacramentally on the altar. R. S. Hawker, the Vicar of Morwenstow in Cornwall, was probably the first to wear this vestment in 1847.[58] But by the mid-1850s there was still only a handful of clergy adopting this practice.

Then in the late 1850s the numbers wearing Eucharistic vestments, lighting candles and eventually burning incense, began to increase rapidly. This was for a number of reasons. For one thing the restoration of existing church buildings, and the building of new ones, had by that point been proceeding for several decades, and the predominant architectural style of most of them was Gothic in imitation of the Middle Ages. John Mason Neale, one of the earliest and most enthusiastic supporters of the Gothic revival, had argued as early as 1843 that as more and more Gothic churches were being restored or built so the demand for the restoration of Gothic vestments would follow as more fitting to the architecture than surplices or gowns.[59] And behind the Gothic revival lay the deep influences of the medievalism of the Romantic movement. In addition, there were more specific reasons, such as the Westerton Judgment in 1857. This was a decision by the Judicial Committee of the Privy Council that certain liturgical practices such as altar frontals and credence tables were legal in the Church of England. This was the first occasion on which a substantial legal judgment had been favourable to High Churchmen, and came as a fillip after previous reverses like the Gorham Judgement.

But perhaps above all it was the steady advance in Eucharistic doctrine within Tractarianism that was the crucial element. As we have seen, it was not until the early 1850s that Robert Wilberforce finally gave a detailed explanation and terminology for such things as the Real Presence and the Eucharistic Sacrifice. This was given added publicity when in 1853–4 Archdeacon Denison preached three sermons in Wells Cathedral with the deliberate intention of testing the acceptability of Wilberforce's concepts in the Church of England. A series of legal cases ensued at both diocesan and archepiscopal level but, to the relief of Tractarians, the case against Denison collapsed on a legal technicality at the beginning of 1858.[60] This led some to argue that if Wilberforce's views were now legitimate, the logical conclusion was to adopt the ritual practices that symbolized them. 'Ritual witnesses to doctrine, and preaches more effectively than the most eloquent of sermons', wrote Charles Le Geyt, a prominent Ritualist, adding that 'without it you cannot teach the Real Presence of our Lord in the Holy Sacrament'.[61] In the 1860s perhaps the most prolific advocate of Ritualism was R. F. Littledale, the incumbent of St Mary the Virgin, Soho, who wrote a series of tracts with titles like *The Christian Sacrifice, The Real Presence* and *The Christian Priesthood* in which he specially associated the Ritualist cause with Eucharistic theology. Wilberforce himself had argued for the eternal presentation of the sacrifice of Christ in heaven and its counterpart in the earthly Eucharist; Le Geyt again took up this concept and applied it to earthly ritual: 'Here is the ritual and worship of heaven. Now, the Church in heaven and the Church on earth corresponds and is united.'[62] Ritual practices now began to advance, and when in 1864 the Scottish Tractarian Bishop Forbes of Brechin attended the consecration of James Skinner's new church at Newland, he described it as being 'like a bit of the Middle Ages let down amongst us'.[63] By the following year B. J. Armstrong estimated that the Eucharistic vestments were in use in some 60 churches.[64] By 1874 the *Tourist's Church Guide* recorded some 136 Ritualist churches using lighted candles and vestments.[65]

How would the older Tractarians react to this new advance by younger men? Over two-thirds of those clergymen recorded as Ritualists in 1874 had been appointed to their parishes since 1860 and clearly represented a new generation.[66] The evidence from the 1860s suggests that there was something of a division in Tractarian ranks on this issue. Some of the older clergy, often after some initial hesitations, themselves began to adopt practices like wearing the Eucharistic vestments. Among these were T. T. Carter, W. J. E. Bennett, James Skinner and J. W. H. Molyneux. But on the other side were others who were not so convinced by the arguments of the Ritualists. William Gresley resigned as Vice President of the English Church Union in 1867 after it openly supported the new ceremonial practices, Thomas Stevens at Bradfield feared for the effects of this type of churchmanship on the boys in his school, B. J. Armstrong worried that it would alienate more parishioners than it could attract, and at Wantage William Butler thought it would be foolish to introduce these new ceremonies before congregations understood the theological principles behind them.[67] They had no theoretical objections to vestments as such, but questioned the pastoral wisdom of introducing them at that stage, before their parishioners were sufficiently prepared either spiritually or practically. As the vestments and ceremonies symbolized a particular view of the Eucharist, was it better to teach the congregation those views first in sermons and classes, or was it better to introduce the vestments first and let understanding grow from the visual appreciation of them? Some of the older Tractarians took the first line, an approach they had adopted at least since the 1840s. The younger Ritualists argued from the analogy of theatres and gin palaces that it was the senses which were affected first, and the understanding would follow [Document 39]. As time passed it was the latter view which prevailed as the numbers of churches employing these ceremonies steadily increased; by 1882 there were 581 churches where candles were lit and 336 in which vestments were worn, and by 1904 the number of Ritualist churches had risen to over 2000.[68]

This had not been achieved without a fight. From the very beginnings of its emergence as an influential force within the Church of England the Evangelicals had opposed Ritualism. On his first acquaintance with a Ritualist service the great Evangelical layman, Lord Shaftesbury, described it as 'the worship of Jupiter and Juno ... such a scene of theatrical gymnastics, of singing, screaming, genuflections ... clouds upon clouds of incense ... one was astounded at the close, that there was no fall of the curtain'.[69] The veteran Evangelical opponent of the Tractarians, Peter Maurice, had no doubt that these new Ritualists were but the latest manifestation of the Popery he had first observed in Oxford in the 1830s [Document 40]. At all events it had to be expunged from the Church of England. In 1865 the Church Association was founded with this objective, and Shaftesbury tabled the first of several Bills in the House of Lords to control the Ritualists with the law. Finally, in 1874, following an inconclusive Royal Commission, the government itself intervened and Parliament passed the Public Worship Regulation Act. Between 1875 and 1890 some eight clergymen were prosecuted, five actually going to prison, although the bishops vetoed a further twelve cases.[70] The attempt to suppress Ritualism by force climaxed in 1890–2 when the saintly Tractarian Bishop of Lincoln, Edward King, was tried by a special episcopal court which largely upheld his innocence, a verdict confirmed by the Judicial Committee of the Privy Council. Legal prosecution had failed to control Ritualism because of a lack of willingness to implement it.[71] As they entered the twentieth century Anglo-Catholics, as they increasingly called themselves, believed they had successfully withstood all that Church and State could do to suppress them, and looked forward to a brighter future.

Epilogue

By the beginning of the twenty-first century the optimism with which Anglo-Catholics had entered the twentieth had receded significantly. During the early decades of the new century Anglo-Catholicism continued its advance in the Church of England, probably reaching a climax in 1933, the centenary of Keble's Assize Sermon, when 50,000 people gathered in the White City Stadium for a Pontifical High Mass.[1] Given the tremendous strides of the previous century it must have seemed only a matter of time before Anglo-Catholics became the dominant force within Anglicanism. But that triumphalism was to be short-lived. In a number of ways the inheritance from the nineteenth century carried within it a series of flaws that were to undermine Anglo-Catholicism in the second half of the twentieth century. The originators of the Oxford Movement believed that the Church of England was the local embodiment of a wider concept of Catholic Christendom, and all they had to do was convince Anglicans of it; hence the initial reaching out to all groups from High Churchmen to Evangelicals. They aimed to make them all aware of their latent Catholicism, not create a Catholic party within a pluralistic Church. The tragedy for them was that what the Tractarians actually helped to bring about was not a unification of Anglicanism but rather an intensification of those very divisions they sought to eradicate. The paradox was that as a small but militant minority the Tractarians were saved by the very tolerance of difference that became a hallmark of modern Anglicanism, a contrast to their own more intolerant stance towards those they disagreed with. As Peter Nockles has commented: 'the result was a sect-like posture and a practical eclecti-cism quite at variance with the original spirit of 1833'.[2] Theologians who had elevated authority within the Church became rebels who defied that authority when they believed their own views were at stake. As the battles and arguments about the legitimacy of Ritu-alism within the Church of England raged in the late 1860s, Henry Manning, by then the Roman Catholic Archbishop of Westminster, put this neatly:

> Ritualism is private judgement in gorgeous raiment ... Every fringe in an elaborate cope worn without authority, is only a distinct and separate act of private judgement; the more elabo-rate, the less Catholic: the nearer the imitation, the further from the submission of faith.[3]

Interestingly, these views have been echoed by a more recent con-vert, the Jesuit Anthony Symondson: 'An Anglo-Catholic under-standing of Catholicism is ultimately established on subjective choice and self-determination ... It is an acceptance of Catholicism founded, ultimately, upon private judgement.'[4] For the early Tractarians private judgement in religious matters was the ultimate manifestation of Protestantism.

As the second half of the twentieth century progressed, all these things came to haunt Anglo-Catholicism. It is arguable that the original Tractarians had seen liberalism as the more potent threat than Protestantism, a theme Newman was to return to in his speech in 1879 when he was created a cardinal: 'For thirty, forty, fifty years I have resisted to the best of my powers the spirit of liberalism in religion', he said, adding: 'Liberalism in religion is the doctrine that there is no positive truth in religion, but that one creed is as good as another ... '[5] In 1889 Charles Gore edited a work on biblical theology called *Lux Mundi,* and in it for the first time theologians within the Anglo-Catholic tradition began to assimilate liberal theology into their thought. By the latter decades of the twentieth century liberalism had become the predominant philo-sophy within academic Anglicanism, and works such as *Honest to God* in 1963, and *The Myth of God Incarnate* in 1977 introduced ideas at a popular level that had become commonplace in university theology departments. The problem for many Anglo-Catholics who still did not share these views was that in a Church of sects tol-eration would have to be extended to all groups, including liberals. The creation of the General Synod in 1970 as the *de facto* legislative body for the Church of England was thus a time bomb waiting to explode. Any legislature is made up of parties or coalitions of parties and once Anglo-Catholics were reduced to a minority that could no longer find allies to join with them, they were in difficulties. The Second Vatican Council in the 1960s had initiated a process of modernization within Roman Catholicism; as High Mass was replaced by folk mass Anglo-Catholic Ritualism began to look outdated and their party a declining relic of past times. In addition, this growing weakness was compounded by the revival of Evangelicalism within the Anglican Church based on the charismatic movement. Then in the late 1970s the Church of England formalized the practice of allowing all Christians of whatever denomination to receive communion in its churches; was this the Church Catholic of the Tractarians, or the national Church of Thomas Arnold?

Finally, in 1992, after years of guerrilla action to prevent it, the General Synod voted to approve the ordination of women. The majority in secular society which had seen women become successful doctors, lawyers or teachers could not see why they should not also be admitted to the clerical profession. In a sense Newman had already answered that in the first of the *Tracts* in 1833 when he had asked the clergy: 'Hitherto you have been upheld by your birth, your education, your wealth, your connexions; should these secular advantages cease, on what must Christ's Ministers depend?' Priesthood is not a job or a profession but a sacrament which cannot be judged in secular terms. The ordination of women went to the heart of the three interconnected fundamentals of Tractarianism: authority, ministry and sacraments. In the face of repeated and detailed warnings from both Rome and Constantinople, representing between them the overwhelming majority of Christians who shared the concept of Apostolic Succession, the Anglican Church presumed an authority to itself alone to radically alter the nature of that Apostolic Ministry. What, then, of St Augustine's words, '*securus judicat orbis terrarum*'? *If* it is impossible for a woman to be a priest, then that in its turn has obvious implications for the validity of the sacraments she celebrates; the potential ordination of women bishops will only compound that. What of the Tractarian assumption 'No bishop, no Church'? And fatally for Anglo-Catholics there can be no escape by blaming the State as with the suppression of the Irish bishoprics in 1833, the Gorham Judgement in 1850, or the Public Worship Regulation Act in 1874. By reducing the role of Parliament within the Ecclesiastical

Establishment and effectively passing legislative functions to the Church itself, (one of the very things nineteenth-century Anglo-Catholics had wanted), a trap of their own desiring had been created for them. Unequivocally the ordination of women is an action originating in the Church herself.

In the decade following the vote in the General Synod some four bishops and several hundred other clergy have left the Church of England, an exodus of High Churchmen unprecedented since the Nonjurors in the late seventeenth century, further weakening the modern Anglo-Catholic party. There can be little doubt that today Anglo-Catholicism is facing its most severe and fundamental crisis. It raises the most searching of questions about the nature of Anglicanism itself. If it *is* the local embodiment of the Catholic Church, as the early Tractarians claimed, would it behave in this way? Were Newman, Ward, Manning and all the others right in the end to abandon Anglicanism for Rome? One of the most flamboyant Anglo-Catholic priests of recent decades, Brian Brindley, explained his departure for Rome in the wake of the ordination of women in a typically light-hearted way, but behind these words is the same dilemma and the same pathos found in many of the crises faced by the Movement since its inception: 'I felt as if I had been a commercial traveller who had been selling vacuum cleaners for 30 years, only to discover suddenly they didn't work.'[6] In 1964 the Vestments of Ministers Measure had finally made the wearing of Eucharistic vestments legal in the Church of England, but at the same time clearly stated that no particular doctrinal significance should be attached to them.[7] To what extent did this symbolize both the success and the failure of the Oxford Movement; had it merely changed the outward appearance of Anglicanism without fundamentally altering the doctrinal ambiguity it had inherited from the Reformation?

Documents

1. A pro-Tractarian history

No story in the whole history of the English Church, since St Augustine landed in AD 597, is so splendid as the history of the Oxford Movement. It has every sort of interest. It is exciting, romantic, chivalrous, like the story of the Crusade. It has its humour as well as its tragedy. And the actors in it were among the most spiritual men who ever lived in England. They were men of genius besides ...

S. L. Ollard, *A Short History of the Oxford Movement* (1915)

2. An anti-Tractarian history

The exposures, herein contained, of the conduct of not a few of the leaders of the Oxford Movement will be unpleasant reading for their followers, as well as for those loyal Churchmen who love honest, straightforward conduct, and hate all crooked ways and double-dealing. It is a sad, though true, story I have to relate. Yet these are days when the truth, however unpleasant, needs to be told without fear or favour, and in the plainest terms.

No candid person who reads this book can fail to see that the destination of the Oxford Movement from its very birth has been Rome. The evidence is too abundant and clear to leave room for doubt.

Walter Walsh, *The History of the Romeward Movement in the Church of England 1833–1864* (1900)

3. The Tractarian view of the eighteenth-century Church

Those who remember the commencement of the century will not need to be reminded of the lifeless condition in which it found the Church of England. Her great material wealth and high secular honours did but add intensity to her spiritual degradation. The sacraments were ministered infrequently, and in the most perfunctory manner. The voice of daily prayer had ceased in almost all churches. The gospel was well nigh banished from the pulpit. The education of the poor was wholly neglected. The missionary functions of the Church were forgotten; although the colonial empire afforded the fairest opening ever offered to any nation for such exertions. Such was the inheritance transmitted to us by a century and a half of worldliness, during which the Church had been content to be the mere tool of the State.

Robert Wilberforce, *A Charge to the Clergy of the East Riding* (1851)

4. An Evangelical praises the *Tracts for the Times*

So wide an influence could never have been exerted, or the approbation, however qualified, of wise and good men have been obtained, unless they had successfully struck some deep chord – had hit on some real wants of the period – and brought out distinctly into light certain substantive principles which, before their appearance, had required an adequate exponent, and had formed none ... They possessed ... occasionally a moving and almost tragic eloquence; and a rich scattering over them of really profound thoughts, which probed unsparingly the religious and political deficiencies of the times.

James Garbutt, *Christ as Prophet, Priest and King* (1842)

5. A radical Dissenter criticizes the Established Church

A reform of the Church, like most other reforms, would permanently benefit the many, and only temporarily injure the few. The lawn-sleeves, the shovel-hats, silk aprons, and monopolising incumbents would be the chief sufferers; while the condition of the most numerous and useful order of the clergy would be improved. Such odious abuses as non-residence and pluralities would be abolished, and the shameful injustice of one man doing the duty and another receiving the reward would be no longer tolerated ...

If the Church is to be saved it must be saved by a wisdom very different from that which directs the councils of the heads of the Establishment. They are obviously as insensible to the position in which they stand as the child unborn ... Ah, my Lords Bishops ... Your days are assuredly numbered; your lease is expired. The fatal vote given in the Reform Bill has sealed your doom, and no depth of repentance can again establish you in the estimation of the people. Solemn pledges will be demanded from a reformed parliament that tithe shall be abolished, and that haughty prelates shall cease to haunt the chambers of legislation. A terrible storm is impending over the Church, and nothing can avert its destructive ravages save a timely abandonment of all that has long excited popular indignation – its enormous wealth – its avarice, pride and self-seeking – its insolent and oppressive power.

John Wade, *The Extraordinary Black Book* (1832)

6. Thomas Arnold's vision of a national Church

This being the state of things, it is evident, that the existence of Dissent has divided the efforts of Christians, so as to make them more adverse to each other than to the cause of ungodliness and wickedness; it has prevented the nation from feeling the full benefits of its national Establishment, and now bids fair to deprive us of them altogether. Dissent, indeed, when it becomes general, makes the Establishment cease to be national; there being so large a portion of the nation whose religious wants it does not satisfy. Yet we have seen, on the other hand, that differences of religious opinion, and of religious rites and ceremonies, are absolutely unavoidable; and that since there exists on earth no infallible authority to decide controversies between Christians, it is vain for any one sect to condemn another, or in its dealings with others to assume that itself is certainly right, and its opponents as certainly in error.

Is it not, then, worth while to try a different system? And since disunion is something so contrary to the spirit of Christianity, and difference of opinion a thing so inevitable to human nature, might it not be possible to escape the former without the folly of attempting to get rid of the latter; to constitute a Church thoroughly national, thoroughly united, thoroughly Christian, which should allow great varieties of opinion, and of ceremonies, and forms of worship, according to the various knowledge, and habits, and tempers of its members, while it truly held one common faith, and trusted in one common Saviour and worshipped one common God?

Thomas Arnold, *Principles of Church Reform* (1833)

7. Romantic poetry at the service of Christianity

Red o'er the forest peers the setting sun,
The line of yellow light dies fast away
That crown'd the eastern copse; and chill and dun
Falls on the moor the brief November day.

Now the tir'd hunter winds a parting note,
And Echo bids good-night from every glade;
Yet wait awhile, and see the calm leaves float
Each to his rest beneath their present shade.

How like decaying life they seem to glide!
And yet no second spring have they in store,
But where they fall, forgotten to abide
Is all their portion, and they ask no more.

Soon o'er their heads blithe April airs shall sing,
A thousand wild-flowers round them shall unfold,
The green buds glisten in the dews of Spring,
And all be vernal rapture as of old.

Unconscious they in waste oblivion lie,
In all the world of busy life around
No thought of them; in all the bounteous sky
No drop, for them, of kindly influence found.

Man's portion is to die and rise again –
Yet he complains, while these unmurmuring part
With their sweet lives, as pure from sin and stain,
As his when Eden held his virgin heart.

And haply half unblam'd his murmuring voice
Might sound in Heaven, were all his second life
Only the first renew'd – the heathen's choice,
A round of listless joy and weary strife.

For dreary were this earth, if earth were all,
Tho' brighten'd oft by dear Affection's kiss; –
Who for the spangles wears the funeral pall?
But catch a gleam beyond it, and 'tis bliss.

John Keble, *The Christian Year* (Twenty-Third Sunday after Trinity) (1827)

8. Newman reviews his life at a moment of crisis for the Church

Lead, kindly Light amid the encircling gloom,
   Lead Thou me on!
The night is dark, and I am far from home –
   Lead thou me on!
Keep thou my feet; I do not ask to see
The distant scene, – one step enough for me.

I was not ever thus, nor prayed that Thou
   Shouldst lead me on.
I loved to choose and see my path; but now,
   Lead Thou me on!
I loved the garish day, and, spite of fears,
Pride ruled my will; remember not past years.

So long Thy power hath blest me, sure it still
   Will lead me on,
O'er moor and fen, o'er crag and torrent, till
   The night is gone;
And with the morn those Angel faces smile
Which I have loved long since, and lost awhile.

John Henry Newman, *Light in the Darkness* (1833)

9. Romanticism and the Eucharist

[W]hat is true of the ordinary services of religion, public and private, holds in a still higher or rather in a special way, as regards the sacramental ordinances of the Church. In these is manifested in greater or less degree, according to the measure of each, that Incarnate Saviour, who is one day to be our Judge, and who is enabling us to bear His Presence then, by imparting it to us in measure now. A thick black veil is spread between this world and the next. We mortal men range up and down it, to and fro, and see nothing. There is no access through it into the next world. In the Gospel this veil is not removed; it remains, but every now and then marvellous disclosures are made to us of what is behind it. At times we seem to catch a glimpse of a form which we shall hereafter see face to face. We approach, and in spite of the darkness, our hands, or our head, or our brow, or our lips become, as it were, sensible of the contact of something more than earthly. We know not where we are, but we have been bathing in water, and a voice tells us that it is blood. Or we have a mark signed upon our foreheads, and it spake of Calvary. Or we recollect a hand laid upon our heads, and surely it had the print of nails in it, and resembled His who with a touch gave sight to the blind and raised the dead. Or we have been eating and drinking; and it was not a dream surely, that One fed us from His wounded side, and renewed our nature by the heavenly meat He gave. Thus in many ways He, who is Judge to us, prepares us to be judged, – He, who is to glorify us, prepares us to be glorified, that He may not take us unawares; but that when the voice of the Archangel sounds, and we are called to meet the Bridegroom, we may be ready.

John Henry Newman, *Worship, a Preparation for Christ's Coming* (1838)

10. The positive impact of the *Tracts for the Times*

It was while we were thus floating without authority to guide us, that the Oxford tracts appeared. It is impossible to exaggerate the immediate effect. In reading them as they came put, one felt a sense of interest and earnestness in religious doctrines one had not known before. Doctrines new to one were vividly taught, and those with which one was familiar, but had held in a somewhat perfunctory

way, started into fresh life. The Church, its Priesthood and Sacraments, acquired a reality unfelt before. Calls then came from
Oxford to vote on critical questions, and then one met old friends
and talked over the new teaching. 'Have you read the tract on
Apostolic Succession? What does it mean?' I remember asking. All
questions seemed to present themselves in a new way.

W. H. Hutchings, *Life and Letters of Thomas Thellusson Carter*
(1904)

11. A critical reaction to the *Tracts for the Times*

A highly respectable, learned and devout class of men has arisen up
at one of our Universities, the tendency of whose writings is
departure from Protestantism, and approach to papal doctrine.
They publish 'tracts for the times' and while they oppose the most
glaring part of popery, – the infallibility of the Pope, the worship of
images, transubstantiation and the like, – yet, though the spirit of
the times is marked by the opposite fault, the very principles of
popery are brought forward by them, under deference to human
authority, especially that of the Fathers: overvaluing the Christian
ministry and sacraments and undervaluing justification by faith.
With much learning and study of the Fathers, with great apparent
and in some cases real devotion and a devotedness ascetic and
peculiar, they seem ... to open another door to the land of darkness
and shadow of death, where the Man of Sin reigns.

Edward Bickersteth, *Remarks on the Progress of Popery* (1836)

12. The usurpations of the State, and the role of the Church

Are we content to be accounted the mere creation of the State, as
schoolmasters and teachers may be, or soldiers, or magistrates, or
other public officers? Did the State make us? can it unmake us? can
it send out missionaries? can it arrange dioceses? Surely all these are
spiritual functions; and Laymen may as well set about preaching,
and consecrating the Lord's Supper, as assume these. I do not say
the guilt is equal; but that, if the latter is guilt, the former is. Would
St. Paul, with his good will, have suffered the Roman power to
appoint Timothy, bishop of Miletus, as well as of Ephesus? Would

Timothy at such a bidding have undertaken the charge? Is not the notion absurd? Yet has it not been realised in what has lately happened? For in what is the English State at present different from the Roman formerly? Neither can be accounted members of the Church of Christ. No one can say the British Legislature is in our communion, or that its members are necessarily even Christians. What pretence then has it for not merely advising, but superseding the Ecclesiastical power?

Bear with me, while I express my fear, that we do not, as much as we ought, consider the force of that article of our Belief, 'The One Catholic and Apostolic Church'. This is a tenet so important as to have been in the Creed from the beginning. It is mentioned there as a *fact*, and a fact *to be believed*, and therefore practical. Now what do we conceive is meant by it? As people vaguely take it in the present day, it seems only an assertion that there is a number of sincere Christians scattered through the world. But is not this a truism? Who doubts it? Who can deny that there are people in various places who are sincere believers? What comes of this? How is it important? Why should it be placed as an article of faith, after the belief in the Holy Ghost? Doubtless the only true and satisfactory meaning is that which our Divines have ever taken, that there is on earth an existing Society, Apostolic as founded by the Apostles, Catholic because it spreads its branches in every place, i.e. the Church Visible with its Bishops, Priests and Deacons. And this surely *is* a most important doctrine; for what can be better news to the bulk of mankind than to be told that Christ when He ascended, did not leave us orphans, but appointed representatives of Himself to the end of time?

John Henry Newman, *Tracts for the Times*, no. 2, 'The Catholic Church' (1833)

13. The Church Visible and Invisible

The Visible Church of God is that one only company which Christians know as yet; it was set up at Pentecost, with the Apostles for founders, their successors for rulers, and all professing Christian people for members. In this Visible Church the Church Invisible is gradually moulded and matured. It is formed slowly and variously by the Blessed Spirit of God, in the instance of this man and that, who belong to the general body. But all these blessed fulfilments of

God's grace are as yet but parts of the Visible Church; they grow from it; they depend upon it; they do not hang upon each other; they do not form a body together; there is no Invisible Church yet formed; it is but a name as yet; a name given to those who are hidden, and known to God only, and as yet but half formed, the unripe and gradually ripening fruit which grows on the stem of the Church Visible. As well might we attempt to foretell the blossoms which will at length turn to account and ripen for the gathering, and then counting up all these and joining them together in our minds, call them by the names of a tree, as attempt now to associate in one the true elect of God. They are scattered about amid the leaves of that Mystical Vine which is seen, and receive their nurture from its trunk and branches. They live on its Sacraments and its Ministry; they gain light and salvation from its rites and ordinances; they communicate with each other through it; they obey its rules; they walk together with its members; they do not dare to judge of this man or that man, on their right hand or their left, whether or not he is absolutely of the number of those who shall be saved; they accept all as their brethren in Christ, as partakers of the same general promises, who have not openly cast off Christ – as really brethren, till death comes, as those are who fulfil their calling most strictly.

John Henry Newman, *The Visible Church an Encouragement to Faith* (1834)

14. Newman looks for a new Athanasius to save the Church

And so of the present perils, with which our branch of the Church is beset, as they bear a marked resemblance to those of the fourth century, so are the lessons, which we gain from that ancient time, especially cheering and edifying to Christians of the present day. Then as now, there was the prospect, and partly the presence in the Church, of an Heretical Power enthralling it, exerting a varied influence and a usurped claim in the appointment of her function-aries, and interfering with the management of her internal affairs. Now as then, 'whatsoever shall fall upon this stone, shall be broken, but on whomsoever it shall fall, it will grind him to powder'. Meanwhile, we may take comfort in reflecting, that, though the present tyranny has more of insult, it has hitherto had less of scandal, than attended the ascendancy of Arianism; we may rejoice in the piety, prudence, and varied graces of our Spiritual Rulers;

and may rest in the confidence, that, should the hand of Satan press us sore, our Athanasius and Basil will be given us in their destined season, to break the bonds of the Oppressor, and let the captives go free.

John Henry Newman, *The Arians of the Fourth Century* (1834)

15. Doctrines lie dormant in the Church

Laicus: I think I quite understand the ground you take. You consider that, as time goes on, fresh and fresh articles of faith are necessary to secure the Church's purity, according to the rise of successive heresies and errors. These articles are all hidden, as it were, in the Church's bosom, from the first, and brought out into form according to the occasion. Such was the Nicene explanation against Arius; the English Articles against Popery: and such are those now called for in this Age of Schism, to meet the new heresy, which denies the holy Catholic Church.

John Henry Newman, *Tracts for the Times*, no. 41, '*Via Media* No. II' (1834)

16. The Eucharist as the centre of Christian worship

The Sacrament of the Lord's Supper, professing as it does to feed us with the Bread of life, and to make us spiritual partakers of the Body and Blood of Christ, ought, one would think, in all reason to form the most prominent feature in the worship of the faithful; to be dwelt on as the sure and abiding pledge of God's love, and sought for earnestly, if possible, as the daily, or at any rate, the weekly sustenance of souls hungry and thirsty after righteousness. One would expect to find those who from circumstances were detained from every other Service, yet, at least, endeavouring to present themselves at this; if necessity compelled them to forego some part of the appointed instruction of the Church, rather one would imagine ought it to be any part than the most solemn and important of all. Churches might be empty, or thinly attended, during the celebration of every other rite: the prayers, the litany, and sermon might be attended only by persons who, from station or accident, were disengaged from necessary occupations: but the Holy

Mystery of our religion, that solemn rite at which is distributed the blessed Bread which came down from heaven, this, at least, should be a signal for the general assemblage of Christ's flock, not, as it now unhappily is, for their dispersion.

Richard Hurrell Froude, *Essay on Rationalism* (1834)

17. Newman reluctant to define Christ's presence in the Eucharist

He says He will give us His flesh to eat. How is this done? We do not know. He gives it under the outward symbols of bread and wine. But in what real sense is the consecrated bread His body? It is not told us, we may not enquire. We say indeed *spiritually, sacramentally, in a heavenly way*; but this is in order to impress on our minds religious, and not carnal notions of it. All we are concerned to know is, *the effect* upon us of partaking this blessed food ... Bread sustains us in this *temporal* life; the consecrated bread is the means of *eternal* strength for soul and body. Who could live this visible life without earthly food? And in the same general way the Supper of the Lord is the *'means'* of our living for ever. We have no reason for thinking we shall live for ever unless we eat it, no more than we have reason to think our temporal life will be sustained without meat and drink. God *can,* indeed, sustain us, 'not by bread alone'; but this is His *ordinary* means, which His will has made such. He can sustain our immortality without the Christian Sacraments, as He sustained Abraham and the other saints of old time; but under the Gospel these are His *means*, which He appointed at His will. We eat the sacred bread, and our bodies become sacred; they are not ours; they are Christ's; they are instinct with that flesh which saw no corruption; they are inhabited by His Spirit; they become immortal; they die but to appearance, and for a time; they spring up when their sleep is ended, and reign with Him for ever.

John Henry Newman, *The Resurrection of the Body* (1832)

18. The earthly Eucharist as the counterpart to the worship of heaven

But if a present work is transacted on our behalf in the Gospel Kingdom, through the merit of Christ's ascended manhood, some means must be appointed, through which His brethren may partake its benefits. A system of worship upon earth is the necessary correlative to a work of intercession in heaven. The one implies the other. And, therefore, in that early age of the Church, when Our Lord's Mediation was felt to be the life of the Christian community, there was a universal and unqualified assertion, that as certainly as Christ's sacrifice was pleaded effectually above, it was likewise truly participated in Gospel ordinances, and that those things which were done on earth in the Church's acts, made part of that grand sacrifice which has its consummation in heaven. So that while all other parts of the Christian Ritual were spoken of as sacrificial in their character, that service by which men especially participated in the Mediation of Christ, because they are most truly bound by it to His mystic body, i.e. the Eucharist or Lord's Supper, was called emphatically the Christian sacrifice. And this is an act which, by its federal character, involves the necessity of that united worship, whereby men partake in the collective privileges of the Church of God ...

Now, it is because what is pleaded above as the ground of our acceptance is that true manhood which was taken for the purpose of Mediation by the Son of God, that the Eucharist, rather than any other part of the Church's Ritual, is declared to be the Christian sacrifice. For 'as often as ye eat this bread and drink this cup, ye do show the Lord's death till he come'. Through its character as a sacrament ... does the Holy Communion connect us with that slain Humanity of the Incarnate Word, which is present by spiritual power in holy ordinances. Through this bread and this cup, that which is offered as a true sacrifice in heaven, is present as a real though immaterial agent in the Church's ministrations. So that what is done by Christ's minister below, is a constituent part of that general work which the one great High Priest performs in heaven: through the intervention of His heavenly head, the earthly sacrificer truly exhibits to the Father that body of Christ, which is the one only sacrifice for sins; each visible act has its efficacy through those visible acts of which it is the earthly expression; and things done on earth are one with those done in heaven.

Robert Isaac Wilberforce, *The Doctrine of the Incarnation of our Lord Jesus Christ* (1849)

19. Pusey on the awfulness of sin

My dear wife's illness first brought to me, what has since been deepened by the review of my past life, how, amid special mercies and guardianship of God, I am scarred all over and seamed with sin, so that I am a monster to myself; I loathe myself; I can feel of myself only like one covered with leprosy from head to foot; guarded as I have been, there is no one with whom I do not compare myself, and find myself worse than they; and yet, thus wounded and full of sores, I am so shocked at myself that I dare not lay my wounds bare to any one ... ; and so I go on, have no such comfort as in good Bishop Andrewes' words, to confess myself 'an unclean work, a dead dog, a putrid corpse', and pray to Him to heal my leprosy as He did on earth, and to raise me from the dead: to give me sight, and to forgive me the 10,000 talents ...

Letter of Edward Bouverie Pusey to John Keble 1844

20. A Tractarian attacks the Evangelicals

All this is substituting a system of man's own creation for that which God has given. Instead of the sacraments and external ordinances, it has put forth prominently a supposed sense of the Atonement, as the badge of a profession. That which is most thoroughly internal, most thoroughly spiritual, secret, and holy, it has made the external symbol of agreement; and therefore has completely (so to speak) turned people inside out, wherever it is received: and thus it has lost the essential peculiarity of Christianity, that purity of heart which is directed to 'the Eye that seeth in secret'.

Isaac Williams, *Tracts for the Times*, no. 87, 'On Reserve in Communicating Religious Knowledge' (1840)

21. A description of Newman preaching

Newman described closely some of the incidents of our Lord's passion; he then paused. For a few moments there was a breathless silence. Then, in a low, clear voice, of which the faintest vibration was audible in the farthest corner of St. Mary's, he said, 'Now, I bid you recollect that He to whom these things were done was Almighty God.' It was as if an electric stroke had gone through the Church, as if every person present understood for the first time the meaning of what he had all his life been saying. I suppose it was an epoch in the mental history of more than one of my Oxford contemporaries.

James Anthony Froude, 'The Oxford Counter Reformation' from *Short Studies on Great Subjects* (1883)

2. Newman's own account of his first doubts about Anglicanism

The Long Vacation of 1839 began early. There had been a great many visitors to Oxford from Easter to Commemoration; and Dr. Pusey's party had attracted attention, more, I think, than in any former year. I had put away from me the controversy with Rome for more than two years. In my Parochial Sermons the subject had at no time been introduced: there had been nothing for two years, either in my Tracts or in the British Critic, of a polemical character. I was returning, for the vacation, to the course of reading which I had many years before chosen as especially my own. I have no reason to suppose that the thoughts of Rome came across my mind at all. About the middle of June I began to study and master the history of the Monophysites. I was absorbed in the doctrinal question. This was from about June 13th to August 30th. It was during this course of reading that for the first time a doubt came upon me of the tenableness of Anglicanism. I recollect on the 30th of July mentioning to a friend, whom I had accidentally met, how remarkable the history was; but by the end of August I was ser-iously alarmed ...

My stronghold was antiquity; now here, in the middle of the fifth century, I found, as it seemed to me, Christendom of the sixteenth and the nineteenth centuries reflected. I saw my face in that mirror, and I was a Monophysite. The Church of the *Via Media* was in the position of the Oriental communion, Rome was where she now is; and the Protestants were the Eutychians ...

Hardly had I brought my course of reading to a close, when the Dublin Review of that August was put into my hands, by friends who were more favourable to the cause of Rome than I was myself. There was an article in it on the 'Anglican Claim' by Dr. Wiseman. This was about the middle of September. It was on the Donatists, with an application to Anglicanism. I read it, and did not see much in it. The Donatist controversy was known to me for some years, as has appeared already. The case was not parallel to that of the Anglican Church. St. Augustine in Africa wrote against the Donatists in Africa. They were a furious party who made a schism within the African Church, and not beyond its limits. It was a case of Altar against Altar, of two occupants of the same See, as that between the Non-jurors in England and the Established Church; not the case of one Church against another, as of Rome against the Oriental Monophysites. But my friend, an anxiously religious man, now, as then, very dear to me, a Protestant still, pointed out the palmary words of St. Augustine, which were contained in one of the extracts made in the Review, and which had escaped my observation. 'Securus judicat orbis terrarum.' He repeated these words again and again, and, when he was gone, they kept ringing in my ears. 'Securus judicat orbis terrarum'; they were words which went beyond the occasion of the Donatists: they applied to that of the Monophysites. They gave a cogency to the Article, which had escaped me at first. They decided ecclesiastical questions on a simpler rule than that of antiquity; nay, St.Augustine was one of the prime oracles of antiquity; here then Antiquity was deciding against itself ... who can account for the impressions which are made on him? For a mere sentence, the words of St. Augustine, struck me with a power which I never had felt from any words before ... 'Securus judicat orbis terrarum!' By those great words of the ancient Father, interpreting and summing up the whole and varied course of ecclesiastical history, the theory of the *Via Media* was absolutely pulverised.

John Henry Newman, *Apologia Pro Vita Sua. Being a History of his Religious Opinions* (1864)

23. The final end of Tractarianism is Roman Catholic doctrine

When the eyes of certain English Churchmen were opened by God's grace some twelve years ago, to discern the fearful precipice towards which religious opinion was hastening among us, they altogether eschewed the idle and ridiculous child's play of examining between rival doctrines by means of patristic and scholastic studies. Had *such* been their course, our Church might have been finally ruined, while they were sitting at home and making up their mind. No! they saw at once that *authority* was the element which was wanting, and they stepped forward as advocates for authority. There *was* a recognised and standard *principle* of authority in the English Church; to that they appealed, – on that as on a firm basis they took their stand, – on that they planted the lever which, so they hoped, might disturb, overthrow, revolutionise, the system then dominant in the Church ...

And what has been the result of this most pious and religious procedure? The course of rationalism has been driven backward with triumph and irresistible might; for though it may have disclosed its real features far more unreservedly and undisguisedly than hitherto it had done, this was the very result of its conflict with those high principles, which now crossed its path: again, the emptiness, hollowness, folly, laxity, unreality of English Protestantism has been held up to light, as it never had been before; a frank and uncompromising defiance has been hurled against it; a whole range of ideas, which had appeared to be finally banished from our theology, have returned among us, with a constraining power and persuasiveness, with an intensity and wide reach of influence, which we have never witnessed since the Reformation; event has succeeded event with such breathless rapidity, that the very principal actors have been startled and bewildered at the fruit of their own labours. While on the other hand, the principles, which have been throughout the centre, rallying-point, and spring of the exertions that have been made, – these have so fruitfully expanded and germinated in the mind of many who had embraced them, that we find, oh most joyful, most wonderful, most unexpected sight! We find the whole cycle of Roman doctrine gradually possessing numbers of English Churchmen; numbers even of those, who are as yet unconscious how much of truth they hold, and may remain so, unless some sudden crisis call on them to make an election and to take a side ...

Three years have passed, since I said plainly, that in subscribing the Articles I renounce no one Roman doctrine: yet I retain my Fellowship which I hold on the tenure of subscription, and have received no Ecclesiastical censure in any shape. It may be said, indeed, that individual Bishops have spoken against those opinions:

but where does the Institution of our Church give individual Bishops any power of authoritatively declaring Church-of-England doctrine? The answer is not doubtful: and while so 'extreme' are the opinions which receive the fullest toleration in our Church, the numbers are daily increasing who consciously embrace them: while still more abundant is the stream of those, who, consciously or unconsciously, are ever pressing in the same direction; and pressing, not by means of independent examination and argumentative enquiry, (which would lead them to error as probably as to truth,) but by means of the surest guides towards sympathy with saintly men and with Rome – habitual watchfulness of conscience, frequent prayer, ever increasing humility, a trust, more and more undivided, in the mercy of God and in the merits of His Son.

W. G. Ward, *The Ideal of a Christian Church* (1844)

24. The way in which ideas change and develop naturally in the world

It is indeed sometimes said that the stream is clearest near the spring. Whatever use may fairly be made of this image, is does not apply to the history of a philosophy or sect, which, on the contrary, is more equable, and purer, and stronger, when its bed has become deep, and broad, and full. It necessarily rises out of an existing state of things, and, for a time, savours of the soil. Its vital element needs disengaging from what is foreign and temporary, and is employed in efforts after freedom, more vigorous and hopeful as its years increase. Its beginnings are no measure of its capabilities, nor of its scope. At first, no one knows what it is, or what it is worth. It remains perhaps for a time quiescent: it tries, as it were, its limbs, and proves the ground under it, and feels its way. From time to time, it makes essays which fail, and are in consequence abandoned. It seems in suspense which way to go; it wavers, and at length strikes out in one definite direction. In time it enters upon strange territory; points of controversy alter their bearing; parties rise and fall about it; dangers and hopes appear in new relations, and old principles reappear under new forms; it changes with them in order to remain the same. In a higher world it is otherwise; but here below to live is to change, and to be perfect is to have changed often.

John Henry Newman, *An Essay on the Development of Christian Doctrine* (1845)

25. Newman imagines Athanasius coming to nineteenth-century Oxford

Did St. Athanasius or St. Ambrose come suddenly to life, it cannot be doubted what communion they would mistake for their own. All surely will agree that these Fathers, with whatever differences of opinion, whatever protests, if we will, would find themselves more at home with such men as St. Bernard or St. Ignatius Loyola, or with the lonely priest in his lodgings, or the holy sisterhood of mercy, or the unlettered crowd before the altar, than with the rulers or the members of any other religious community. And may we not add, that were the two Saints, who once sojourned, in exile or on embassage, at Treves, to come more northward still, and to travel until they reached another fair city, seated among groves, green meadows, and calm streams, the holy brothers would turn from many a high aisle and solemn cloister which they found there, and ask the way to some small chapel where mass was said in the populous alley or forlorn suburb? And, on the other hand, can any one who has but heard his name, and cursorily read his history, doubt for one instant how the people of England, in turn, 'we, our princes, our priests, and our prophets', Lords and Commons, universities, ecclesiastical courts, marts of commerce, great towns, country parishes, would deal with Athanasius – Athanasius who spent his long years in fighting against kings for a theological term?

John Henry Newman, *An Essay on the Development of Christian Doctrine* (1845)

26. A Tractarian response to Newman's conversion to Roman Catholicism

Why this softening of words? Is it an act of Schism to leave the Communion of the Catholic Church or is it not? If it be, then why not call those who are guilty of the sin by the right name? Whether it be the imaginative Mr. Ward who deals in Ideas; or should it be the subtle Mr. Oakley who holds all Roman doctrine; whether it be the simple Mr. Wingfield who believes the Church to be represented by the individual judge of the Court of Arches and takes his dogmas as though he were a Pope-infallible; or whether (alas!) it should be, as now it is said beyond doubt it is, the learned and pious Mr.

Newman, – still every one is nothing more or less than guilty of Schism. If they depart from us, let them depart: let us grieve for them; let us pray for them; let us fast day and night and offer up bitter cries and supplication to God on their behalf. But let us not deceive ourselves and them by soft words. It is a sin of which they are guilty; and as sinners in that act let us lament for them in common justice to ourselves, for if they are not guilty of sin, in what position are we who remain? Let them depart, but let them not depart as 'Seceders' but as 'Schismatics'.

W. J. E. Bennett, letter to the *English Churchman* (16 October 1845)

27. The arrival of open hostility in a Tractarian parish

Some morning, unexpectedly, and to everyone's astonishment, the whole parish is inundated with some cheap copies of Lord John's Letter to the Bishop of Durham, or something of that kind, headed by some title as 'A knock-down to Puseyites', or, 'A Severe Blow to Tractarians'. The shop windows are filled with rude and blasphemous caricatures and the walls exhibit an abundant display about 'No Popery', 'No Candlesticks', all unusually well written, and all bearing a strong family likeness in the handwriting. The Church is in danger; an immense excitement is got up; petitions are prepared to Queen, Lords, Commons, and all sorts of people. In the midst of all this a Memorial is slipped in to the Bishop, nominally against the Pope, really against the Parson, and in the panic and confusion is signed by nine-tenths of the bewildered, respectable, but not very intelligent inhabitants.

Reginald N. Shutte, *A Memoir of the Late Rev. Henry Newland* (1861)

28. The 'No Popery' cry addressed to parishioners

Sometimes they are exhibited in very large letters on a board, and carried by a poor boy hired (we ought perhaps to say bribed) for the purpose, round the church of St. Peter, and before the doors, at the time of Daily Service. And then this banner, followed by a procession worthy of it, is carried after any persons who it is supposed may be annoyed by it ... Occasionally 'No Popery' is shouted out in the porch of the church during the time of Divine Service. And again, these words ... are heard at midnight sung in chorus by drunken men – literally screamed and yelled – as a novel but most fitting variety amongst their ordinary songs.

J. W. H. Molyneux, *The 'No Popery' Cry, and the Dissenters of Sudbury* (1855)

29. A Tractarian criticizes the middle classes

The real truth is, that our tradesmen, the representatives of that wonderful middle class, which newspapers and officials flatter and imagine to be the most capable of people to rule the country etc., etc., putting all local concerns into their hands, religion, education, sanitary reform, provision for the poor, are a thoroughly ignorant, ungodly set. There are no doubt, and thank God for it, bright exceptions, but the majority care for nothing except keeping up respectability and making money. They smile or sneer at every kind of sin which does not affect life or property. I do not hesitate to say all but entirely without God to the world, i.e. they refer nothing to His Presence, or their duty to Him, but only consider how far it affects their pocket, pleasure, or reputation.

William Butler, *Wantage Parish Diaries* (1 December, 1855)

30. False notions about receiving Holy Communion

It will be found in nearly every part of England, that the prevailing impression is, that there is no necessity laid on them to receive communion, that it is a duty which may be dispensed with safely till death; that it is rather an act intended for the saintly character, than the means necessary for forming it; that the possibility of sinning after communicating is sufficient reason for abstaining, and that the existence of any daily temptation, such as blasphemous conversation of fellow workmen, or the cares of a surrounding family, are direct hindrances to reception.

Edward Monro, *Parochial Work* (1850)

31. More false views of Holy Communion

Ask a parishioner why he abstains himself from the Lord's Table, and he will tell you that he is not fit: the man's idea is, not that his will is indisposed to do the Lord's work, or that he is determined to continue in the practice of some sin of which he is conscious, and that therefore he is not fit to approach his God; his idea is, that he has not yet achieved, by his own unaided efforts, that amount of holiness which would entitle him to God's help – Humbly as his idea is worded, that man's notion of Christianity is salvation by works – the Lord's Supper, whatever be his idea of the benefits received, is payment for work done.

Henry Newland, *Confirmation and First Communion* (1854)

32. Fears about confession and the family

How near the 'circlings of the fatal vortex' those young persons may already be, who have been inadvertently permitted to attend Tractarian churches, their parents are probably but little aware. The Rev. J. C. Miller states that a dignitary of the Church was asked by a young lady whether it was wrong to confess to him without her parents' knowledge. The answer was, that at her age, *silence was the proper course.* The Bishop of Ripon names a clergyman at Leeds who reproved a married woman for mentioning to her husband that she had been to confession, – 'Confession', he said, 'was a thing we ought not to tell the husband; it concerned our souls and not our bodies.' After these significant warnings and the disclosures of the Confessional, as *actually practised in the Church of England,* indifference or connivance on the part of parents or husbands, is without excuse.

Report of the Proceedings of the Brighton Protestant Defence Committee (1854)

33. A deathbed confession

... so alone I was left, and then pursued as the Church directs, an examination of the sick man's faith and life, and exhorted him to confession of his sins. Knowing him from his previous character and life that he had lived, up to his light, a life of moral holiness, at least for many years, and hearing what he had to say of the follies and sins of his youth; then comforting and directing him as best I could, and believing fully that ALMIGHTY GOD would receive his confession and his penitence, I pronounced over him the Absolution of the Church. I then left him quite composed and tranquil.

W. J. E. Bennett, *The Old Church Porch*, vol. IV (1 October 1860)

34. Confession in practice

I had had much talk with her on the subject of Confession and Absolution as the best means of obtaining the peace of mind for which she craved, and lately especially I brought things to a point. This evening she made as full a confession as one in her circumstances of health and education, brought up as our folk are, could do, and expect the greatest thankfulness and comfort after absolution given.

William Butler, *Wantage Parish Diaries* (20 July 1857)

35. The social consequences of pews

The world has come into our churches to mark out too distinctly the RICH and the POOR, where RELIGION only in former times distinguished the holy from the unholy. Now the naves of our churches are too much secularised and defaced by *pews*, marking out the wealthy and the great; and open seats marking out the poor ... No, this *cannot be right*.

W. J. E. Bennett, *The Principles of the Book of Common Prayer Considered* (1845)

36. A comparison of pews and vaults

We ascribe vaults to the state of mind engendered by pues. Rather, perhaps, we should ascribe pues and vaults to the natural effects of the same anti-Christian spirit ... It may be urged, indeed, that the pue holder may lock up his pue and absent himself from church; in which case he will merit a more severe judgement than the owner of the vault, who cannot but occupy it; but on the other hand, we answer that the holder of the pue pretends to claim his church room no longer than during the term of his natural life, whereas the builder of a vault does what he can to keep *his* churchroom for ever.

The Ecclesiologist, vol. IV (1845)

37. The reaction of the poor to pews

... they find the church full of pews or benches allotted to a limited number of 'respectable' people; into whose private seats they shrink from intruding, and from which they are in fact repelled by all the conventionalities and distinctions of worldly life; and, in striking contrast, a few pauper seats set apart from them, to which alone they are welcome.

J. W. H. Molyneux, *A Letter Addressed to the Lord Bishop of Ely, on the Equal Rights of all Classes of Parishioners to the Use of the Parish Church, and the Unchristian Results of the Appropriation of Seats* (1856)

38. Fictional advice to the clergy

One man will go to a neglected parish, and revive daily service, before his flock has learned to be thankful that the church is open twice instead of once on a Sunday: a second, on arriving at a place full of Dissenters, will, in his love of antiquity (or notoriety), attempt the restoration of some usage long laid aside, or for which there is no very direct authority in our formularies, and thus lay himself open to the charges of Popery, and so forth: a third, with right feelings but unsound judgement, will do some act (right in itself, but injudicious from the circumstances or period of its adoption) which will make his parishioners suspicious of his principles, though, if he would only have been content to wait a little until he was known, it might have been done with great advantage.

F. E. Paget, *Milford Malvoisin: or, Pews and Pewholders* (1842)

39. The attractions of gin palaces compared to Ritualism

There is no institution so widely and universally popular amongst the London poor as the gin-palace. Given the craving for drink, and it would seem that no additional inducement would be needful to lure customers across the threshold, and to retain them as long as possible on the premises. Yet it is not so. A gin-palace, whose entrance is up a couple of steps from the footway, or whose doors do not swing open readily at a touch, is at a commercial disadvantage when compared with others on the street level and with patent hinges. Nay, more, internal decoration, abundant polished metal and vivid colour, with plenty of bright light, is found to pay, and to induce people to stay on drinking, just because everything is so pretty and cheerful to the eye, and so unlike the squalid discomfort of their own sordid homes. Many landlords have found even all this insufficient, without the additional attraction of music; and the low singing-hall is sure to indicate the most thriving drinking-shops in the worst quarters of the metropolis. If, then, painting, light, and music are found necessary adjuncts to a trade which already has enlisted on its side one of the strongest of human passions, it is the most besotted folly to reject their assistance, when endeavouring to persuade men to accept and voluntarily seek an article for which they have never learnt to care, even if they are not actively hostile to it – to wit, Religion.

R. F. Littledale, *The Missionary Aspects of Ritualism* (1866)

40. Tractarianism leads to Ritualism

... at length Tractarianism, which (according to Dr. Pusey's own favourite illustration) was only the bulb, sprung up into Ritualism as the flower of the day that was to be the pride of their fleeting summer ... From the consecration of the model Chapel of St.

Mary's, at Littlemore, in September, 1836, to the dedication of the monster Mass House at St. Bartholomew, at Brighton, in the year 1874, there would be little difficulty in tabulating the variations of the ecclesiastical thermometer; and we should thus be enabled to follow out the fitful course of the Ritual Christian year, – from the dry, frigid level of an Oxford winter solstice, to the high summer temperature of even sunny Italy herself.

Peter Maurice, *The Ritualists or Non-Natural Catholics* (1874)

Notes

Introduction: interpretations past and present

1. David Bebbington, *Holiness in Nineteenth-Century England: The 1998 Didsbury Lectures* (Carlisle: Paternoster Press, 2000), p. 7.

2. Peter Toon, *Evangelical Theology 1833–1856: A Response to Tractarianism* (London: Marshall, Morgan and Scott, 1979), p. 1.

3. Dorinda Outram, *The Enlightenment* (Cambridge: Cambridge University Press, 1995) especially pp. 1–13 for a discussion of modern views of the Enlightenment.

4. J. H. Newman, *Tracts for the Times*, no. 1, 'Thoughts on the Ministerial Commission Respectfully Addressed to the Clergy' (London: Rivington, 1833), p. 1.

5. J. H. Newman, *Apologia Pro Vita Sua: Being a History of his Religious Opinions* (edited by Martin J. Svaglic, Oxford: Clarendon Press, 1967), p. 43.

6. See, for instance, B. G. Worrall, *The Making of the Modern Church: Christianity in England since 1800* (London: SPCK, 1988), p. 15.

7. Marvin R. O'Connell, *The Oxford Conspirators: A History of the Oxford Movement 1833–1845* (London: University Press of America, 1969).

8. R. W. Church, *The Oxford Movement: Twelve Years 1833–1845* (edited by Geoffrey Best, Chicago: University of Chicago Press, 1970), p. 271.

NOTES

1 Contexts

1. Kenneth Hylson-Smith, *High Churchmanship in the Church of England: From the Sixteenth Century to the late Twentieth Century* (Edinburgh: T&T Clark, 1993), p. 9.

2. See Aidan Nichols, *The Panther and the Hind: A Theological History of Anglicanism* (Edinburgh: T&T Clark, 1993), p. 64.

3. See Peter Benedict Nockles, *The Oxford Movement in Context: Anglican High Churchmanship 1760–1857* (Cambridge: Cambridge University Press, 1994), p. 156.

4. Hylson-Smith, pp. 15 and 17.

5. See ibid. pp. 73–4 and Nichols p. 73.

6. Nockles, pp. 270 and 309.

7. Nichols, p. 77.

8. Hylson-Smith, pp. 101 and 107.

9. Nockles, pp. 271–2.

10. Ibid., p. 274.

11. *Tracts for the Times by Members of the University of Oxford*, vol. I for 1833–4 (London: Rivington, 1840 edition), p. iii.

12. See Nockles, p. 149 for a list of these works.

13. Ibid., p. 127.

14. Out of the first 65 *Tracts* no fewer than 16 are such collections.

15. For a discussion of this, see Nockles, pp. 127 and 136.

16. Newman, *Apologia* p. 478. Sheridan Gilley, *Newman and his Age* (London: Darton, Longman and Todd, 1990), p. 21. See also David Newsome, 'The Evangelical sources of Newman's power', in John Coulson and A. M. Allchin (eds), *The Rediscovery of Newman: An Oxford Symposium* (London: Sheed and Ward/SPCK, 1967).

17. Robert Isaac Wilberforce, *The Evangelical and Tractarian Movements: A Charge to the Clergy of the East Riding, Delivered at the Ordinary Visitation* (London: John Murray, 1851), p. 11.

18. See W. E. Gladstone, *Gleanings of Past Years, 1843–1879* (1879), vii, pp. 232–5; and J. H. Overton, *The Anglican Revival* (1897), p. 15.

19. E. A. Knox, *The Tractarian Movement 1833–1845* (London: Putnam, 1933), p. 53.

20. Toon, p. 17.

21. Ibid., p. 21.

22. Ibid., pp. 23–4.

23. Ibid., p. 32.

24. Ibid., p. 45.

25. Ibid., p. 61.

26. Dieter Voll, *Catholic Evangelicalism: The Acceptance of Evangelical Traditions by the Oxford Movement during the Second Half of the Nineteenth Century* (London: The Faith Press, 1963), p. 35.

27. Yngve Brilioth, *Three Lectures on Evangelicalism and the Oxford Movement* (Oxford: Oxford University Press, 1934), pp. 9–10.

28. I am indebted to Peter Nockles for the discovery of this moving passage. See Nockles, p. 327.

29. Hylson-Smith, p. 104.

30. David Newsome, *The Parting of Friends: A Study of the Wilberforces and Henry Manning* (London: John Murray, 1966), pp. 9–10. See also Toon, pp. 2–3.

31. 1 Corinthians 14: 8.

32. For a discussion of the relations of Church and State in these years see G. I. T. Machin, *Politics and the Churches in Great Britain 1832–1868* (Oxford: Oxford University Press, 1977), pp. 1–27.

33. For some comments on the details of Wade's book see G. M. Ditchfield, *The Evangelical Revival* (London: UCL Press, 1998), pp. 42–3.

34. For an account of the passage of the Bill, see Machin, pp. 31–9.

35. Quoted in A. P. Stanley, *Life and Correspondence of Dr. Arnold* (1844), p. 278.

36. See Thomas Arnold, *Principles of Church Reform* (with an introductory essay by M. J. Jackson and J. Rogan, London: SPCK, 1962), p. 59. This modern edition contains the full text of Arnold's original work.

37. William Gibson, *Church, State and Society 1760–1850* (Basingstoke: Macmillan, 1994), p. 138.

38. Piers Brendon, *Hurrell Froude and the Oxford Movement* (London: Paul Elek, 1974), p. xvii.

39. Hylson-Smith, p. 126.

40. Ibid., p. 130.

41. Newsome, *Parting of Friends*, p. 226.

42. Brendon, p. 190.

43. George H. Tavard, *The Quest for Catholicity: A Study in Anglicanism* (London: Burns and Oates, 1963), p. 179.

44. Newman, *Apologia* p. 42. J. H. Newman and John Keble (eds), *Remains of the Reverend Richard Hurrell Froude*, vol. I. (1838), p. 308.

45. For an account of this campaign, see J. T. Ward, *The Factory Movement 1830–1855* (Newton Abbot: David and Charles, 1962). The full text of Oastler's letter is reproduced in J. T. Ward, *The Factory System*, vol. II. (1970), pp. 73–6.

46. Ward, *Factory Movement*, p. 30.

47. For an account see Nicholas C. Edsall, *The Anti-Poor Law Movement 1834–1844* (Manchester: Manchester University Press, 1971).

48. *Remains*, vol. III., p. 274.

49. Quoted in Brendon, p. 95.

50. Quoted in ibid., p. 132.

51. Ibid., p. 144.

52. *Remains*, vol. I, p. 374.

53. Roy Porter and Mikulas Teich, *Romanticism in National Context* (Cambridge: Cambridge University Press, 1988), p. 4.

54. See Maurice Cranston, *The Romantic Movement* (Oxford: Blackwell, 1994), p. 17.

55. Quoted in ibid.

56. Stephen Prickett, *Romanticism and Religion: The Tradition of Coleridge and Wordsworth in the Victorian Church* (Cambridge: Cambridge University Press, 1976), p. 170. Nichols, p. 118.

57. Geoffrey Rowell, 'John Keble – A Speaking Life', in Charles R. Henery (ed.) *A Speaking Life: John Keble and the Anglican Tradition of Ministry and Art* (Leominster: Gracewing, 1995), p. 52.

58. Prickett, p. 93.

59. See Meriol Trevor, *Newman: The Pillar of the Cloud* (Basingstoke: Macmillan, 1962), p. 138. Gilley, pp. 9 and 102. Ian Ker, *John Henry Newman: A Biography* (Oxford: Clarendon Press, 1988), pp. 79–80.

60. See Prickett, p. 56 for comments on this similarity between Coleridge and Newman.

61. Nockles, p. 325. He refers explicitly to the older High Churchmen, but clearly his comments are also applicable to the Evangelicals.

2 Ideas

1. William Palmer *A Narrative of Events Connected with the publication The Tracts for the Times* (1883 edition) pp. 56–7. This was first published in 1843 but the 1883 edition contains much new material.

2. For details see Ditchfield, p. 100.

3. See Rune Imberg, *In Quest of Authority: The 'Tracts for the Times' and the Development of the Tractarian Leaders 1833–1841* (Lund: Lund University Press, 1987), p. 17.

4. Ibid., pp. 15–16.

5. Ibid., p. 29, note 44.

6. Ibid., p. 28.

7. Newman, *Apologia*, pp. 48–9.

8. Imberg, p. 24.

9. Ibid., pp. 33–4.

10. I am indebted to Peter Toon for this excellent quotation. See Toon, pp. 26–7.

11. See Mats Selen, *The Oxford Movement and Wesleyan Methodism in England 1833–1882: A Study in Religious Conflict* (Lund: Lund University Press, 1992), p. 81.

12. *Tracts*, no. 1. p. 4.

13. See Newsome, *Parting of Friends*, p. 192.

14. For an account of the Tractarian takeover, see Nockles, pp. 277–81.

15. *Tracts*, no. 1, p. 2.

16. See above p. 126, note 48.

17. For a discussion of this see Nockles, especially pp. 79–85.

18. See Toon, p. 173.

19. Ibid., p. 176.

20. Nockles, p. 114.

21. Ibid., pp. 112–13.

22. Stephen Thomas, *Newman and Heresy: The Anglican Years* (Cambridge: Cambridge University Press, 1991), p. 61.

23. Gilley, p. 23.

24. Thomas, p. 34.

25. Newman, *Apologia*, p. 54.

26. Ibid., p. 256.

27. J. H. Newman, 'Tamworth Reading Room', in *Discussions and Arguments on Various Subjects* (1911 edition), pp. 293–5.

28. See Duncan Forbes, *The Liberal Anglican Idea of History* (Cambridge: Cambridge University Press, 1952) p. 103.

29. Thomas, p. 108.

30. See ibid., pp. 117–18.

31. See *Remains*, vol. IV for Froude's account of Becket.

32. Thomas, p. 50 where he seems to agree with this interpretation.

33. *Tracts,* no. 38, p. 6.

34. Ibid., p. 2.

35. Ibid., p. 9.

36. For a discussion of this, see Thomas, p. 185.

37. See Louis Allen, *John Henry Newman and the Abbé Jager: A Controversy on Scripture and Tradition (1834–1836)* (Oxford: Oxford University Press, 1975).

38. See for instance Imberg, p. 53 for the editorial changes to the two 'Via Media' *Tracts*, nos. 38 and 41.

39. Nockles, p. 311.

40. *Remains*, vol. I, pp. 336, 389 and 433.

41. See Nockles, pp. 122–7 for comments on the reaction of High Churchmen.

42. See Toon, pp. 118–19, 125 and 130 for details.

43. This is reproduced in full in *Remains*, vol. III.

44. For a discussion of these see Nockles, pp. 235–7; and Alf Härdelin, *The Tractarian Understanding of the Eucharist* (Uppsala: Uppsala University Press, 1965), pp. 123–8.

45. See Härdelin, pp. 134 and 149.

46. Ibid., p. 132.

47. J. H. Newman, *Parochial and Plain Sermons*, vol. VI. (1868), p. 150 (Sermon XI, 'The Eucharistic Presence').

48. Newsome, *Parting of Friends*, p. 373.

49. Härdelin, p. 162.

50. Ibid., p. 142.

51. Ibid., p. 165.

52. Ibid., p. 219.

53. Newsome, *Parting of Friends*, p. 380.

54. Härdelin, p. 166.

55. Nockles, pp. 243–4.

56. Toon, p. 175.

57. Ibid., p. 201.

58. Selen, p. 379.

59. See Ker, *Newman*, p. 4.

60. John Saward, *Perfect Fools* (1980), pp. 203–8. See also Gabriel O'Donnell, 'The Spirituality of E. B. Pusey', in Perry Butler (ed.), *Pusey Rediscovered* (Oxford: Oxford University Press, 1983).

61. *Tracts*, no. 18 p. 12.

62. See Keith Denison, 'Dr. Pusey as Confessor and Spiritual Director', in Butler, p. 215.

63. Ibid., pp. 215–18.

64. For the history of Anglican Religious Communities, see A. M. Allchin, *The Silent Rebellion: Anglican Religious Communities 1845–1900* (London: SCM Press, 1958) and Peter F. Anson, *The Call of the Cloister* (London: SPCK, 1964).

65. Nockles, pp. 248–56.

66. Selen, pp. 187–90.

67. See Nockles, pp. 186–7 for a discussion of High Church reactions to Tractarian enthusiasm.

68. See Brendon, p. 50; O. W. Jones, *Isaac Williams and his Circle* (London: SPCK, 1971), p. 9.

69. Sir George Prevost (ed.), *The Autobiography of Isaac Williams* (second edition, London: Longmans, Green and Co., 1892), p. 19.

70. Nockles, p. 200.

71. Isaac Williams, *Tracts*, no. 87, 'On Reserve in Communicating Religious Knowledge' (London: Rivington, 1840). This is reprinted in part in Elizabeth Jay (ed.), *The Evangelical and Oxford Movements* (Cambridge: Cambridge University Press, 1983), p. 108.

72. Ibid., p. 114.

73. Ibid., p. 115.

74. Ibid., pp. 120–1.

75. Toon, pp. 133–5.

76. For a discussion of the difficulties of defining Puritanism, see P. McGrath, *Papists and Puritans Under Elizabeth I* (London: Batsford, 1967), pp. 31–46.

3 Events

1. F. L. Cross, *John Henry Newman* (London: Allan, 1933), Appendix IV, 'The Myth of July 14, 1833', pp. 162–3.

2. Louis Bouyer, *Newman: His Life and Spirituality* (London: Burns and Oates, 1958), p. 152.

3. Nockles, p. 69.

4. Brendon, pp. 94–9.

5. Thomas, p. 20.

6. See Nockles, p. 36, and Toon, p. 29.

7. See Nockles, p. 36.

8. See Brendon, p. 42, and Toon, p. 139.

9. Nockles, p. 38.

10. Ibid., p. 36. Also Owen Chadwick, 'The Oxford Movement and its Reminiscencers' (1983), in *The Spirit of the Oxford Movement* (Cambridge: Cambridge University Press, 1990), pp. 135–6.

11. Henry Newland, *Three Lectures on Tractarianism* (London: Masters, 1852).

12. Chadwick, p. 136.

13. Nockles, pp. 41–2.

14. Chadwick, p. 136.

15. See e.g. Geoffrey Rowell, *The Vision Glorious: Themes and Personalities of the Catholic Revival in Anglicanism* (Oxford: Oxford University Press, 1983).

16. See Brendon, p. 68.

17. Ibid., p. 84.

18. Gilley, p. 3.

19. Meriol Trevor, *Newman: The Pillar of the Cloud* and *Newman: Light in Winter* (Basingstoke: Macmillan, 1962).

20. See Gilley, pp. 44, 50 and 53.

21. See Newsome, *Parting of Friends*, p. 30.

22. See Prevost, *Autobiography*, pp. 70–2.

23. Newman, *Apologia*, p. 64.

24. Imberg, pp. 164–5.

25. Ibid., pp. 166–9.

26. Ibid., pp. 171–2.

27. Ibid., pp. 174–6.

28. Ibid., p. 163.

29. Prevost, *Autobiography*, p. 70.

30. Rowell, *Vision Glorious*, p. 80.

31. Norman Gash, *Peel* (London: Longman, 1976), p. 4.

32. Brendon, p. 128.

33. Ian Ker (ed.), *Letters and Diaries of John Henry Newman*, vol. IV (Oxford: Oxford University Press, 1979), p. 69.

34. Ker, *Newman*, p. 101.

35. Newsome, *Parting of Friends*, p. 339.

36. Toon, pp. 23–4.

37. Nockles, pp. 274–7.

38. Brendon, pp. 181 and 184.

39. Ibid., p. 184.

40. Nockles, p. 282.

41. Gilley, p. 165.

42. Imberg, p. 134.

43. Ibid., p. 53.

44. Ibid., pp. 139–40.

45. Gilley, p. 155.

46. Thomas, p. 205.

47. Ibid., p. 206.

48. Ibid., p. 208.

49. Ibid., pp. 215 and 217.

50. Ibid., p. 220.

51. Ibid., pp. 218 and 226.

52. Gilley, p. 200.

53. Quoted in Toon, p. 185.

54. Gilley, p. 207.

55. Nockles, pp. 308–9.

56. Chadwick, pp. 151–2.

57. Nockles, p. 129.

58. Church, p. 271; S. L. Ollard, *A Short History of the Oxford Movement* (London: Mowbray, 1915), p. 105.

59. C. P. S. Clarke, *The Oxford Movement and After* (London: Mowbray, 1932), p. 130.

60. Newsome, *Parting of Friends*, p. 195.

61. Keble's letter is quoted in Georgina Battiscombe, *John Keble: A Study in Limitations* (London: Constable, 1963), pp. 260–2.

62. Clarke, p. 130.

63. A. Clifton Kelway, *George Rundle Prynne* (London: Longmans, Green and Co., 1905), pp. 12–14 and 16–17.

64. [Maria Trench] *James Skinner: A Memoir* (London: Kegan, Paul and Trench, 1883), pp. 18 and 21.

65. J. F. Briscoe and H. F. B. Mackay, *A Tractarian at Work: A Memoir of Dean Randall* (London: Mowbray, 1932), pp. 34 and 49.

66. See C. Moor, *A Short Account of the Family of Stevens* (Kendal: Titus Wilson and Son, 1918) for a history of the family.

67. A. J. Butler, *Life and Letters of William John Butler* (London: Macmillan, 1897), p. 25.

68. W. H. Hutchings, *Life and Letters of Thomas Thellusson Carter* (London: Longmans Green and Co., 1904), pp. 8–9 and 14. See also Document No. 10.

69. Eleanor A. Towle, *John Mason Neale: A Memoir* (London: Longman, 1906), pp. 30 and 38.

70. F. Bennett, *The Story of W. J. E. Bennett* (London: Longmans, Green and Co., 1909), pp. 9–10 and 33; and W. J. E. Bennett, *A Farewell Letter to his Parishioners* (London: Cleaver, 1851), p. 5.

71. G. A. Denison, *Notes of My Life, 1805–1878* (1878), pp. 66–7.

72. Newland, *Three Lectures*, pp. 86 and 91.

73. William Gresley, *Bernard Leslie: or, A Tale of the Last Ten Years* (London: James Burns, 1843), especially pp. 129, 234, and 294.

74. William Gresley, *A Third Statement of the Real Danger of the Church of England* (London: James Burns, 1847), p. 20.

75. G. W. Herring, *Tractarianism to Ritualism: A Study of Some Aspects of Tractarianism outside Oxford, from the Time of Newman's Conversion in 1845, until the First Ritual Commission in 1867* (Oxford

D.Phil thesis, 1984). Appendix 'A Table of Tractarian Clergy from 1840 to 1870'.

76. Henry Parry Liddon, *Life of Edward Bouverie Pusey* (four volumes, London: Longmans, 1893–1897), vol. II, p. 461.

77. Towle, p. 133.

78. See Herring, pp. 29–32.

79. William Gresley, *A Second Statement on the Real Danger of the Church of England* (London: James Burns, 1847), pp. 12 and 69–70; and *The Real Danger of the Church of England* (London: James Burns, 1846), p. 8.

4 Parishes

1. Alan Haig, *The Victorian Clergy* (London: Croom Helm, 1984), Table 1.1, p. 3.

2. See B. I. Coleman, *The Church of England in the Mid-Nineteenth Century: A Social Geography* (London: Historical Association, 1980) and John D. Gay, *The Geography of Religion in England* (London: Duckworth, 1971).

3. The fullest account of this is G. F. A. Best, *Temporal Pillars: Queen Anne's Bounty, the Ecclesiastical Commissioners, and the Church of England* (Cambridge: Cambridge University Press, 1964).

4. Quoted in Desmond Bowen, *The Idea of the Victorian Church: A Study of the Church of England 1833–1889* (Montreal: McGill University Press, 1968), p. 21.

5. Bernarr Rainbow, *The Choral Revival in the Anglican Church (1839–1872)* (New York: Oxford University Press, 1970), p. 174.

6. James Obelkevitch, *Religion and Rural Society: South Lindsey 1825–1875* (Oxford: Clarendon Press, 1976), p. 108.

7. E. R. Norman, *Anti-Catholicism in Victorian England* (London: Allen and Unwin, 1968), p. 64.

8. W. J. E. Bennett, *A First Letter to the Right Honourable Lord John Russell* (1850), pp. 4–5.

9. *Memorial of the Churchwardens of the Parish of Westbourne* (1851), p. 22.

10. Butler, *Life of Butler* (1897), p. 85.

11. Ibid., p. 85; William Butler, *Wantage Parish Diaries*, 1 April 1852.

12. David Roberts, *Paternalism in Early Victorian England* (London: Croom Helm, 1979), pp. 105–28 and 180–3.

13. See especially R. A. Soloway, *Prelates and People: Ecclesiastical Social Thought in England 1783–1857* (London: RKP, 1969), pp. 186, 260–1, 320 and 333–40.

14. W. E. Heygate, *Care of the Soul* (London: Rivington, 1851), p. 109.

15. See William Gresley, *Parochial Sermons* (1842) p. ix, and W. J. E. Bennett, *Calling Upon God* (1849), p. 18.

16. See e.g. John Mason Neale, *Ayton Priory; or, the Restored Monastery* (London: Deightons, 1843), and William Gresley, *Colton Green: A Tale of the Black Country* (1846).

17. See Trench, *Skinner Memoir*, pp. 202–3.

18. Thomas Stevens, *Letter Books*, 4 April 1850 and 26 March 1851 (unpublished MS).

19. Herbert B. J. Armstrong (ed.), *Armstrong's Norfolk Diary. Further Passages from the Diary of the Rev. Benjamin John Armstrong, Vicar of East Dereham 1850–1888* (London: Hodder and Stoughton, 1963), p. 31.

20. W. E. Heygate, *William Blake: or, the English Farmer* (London: Masters, 1848), p. v.

21. Ibid., pp. 9–10.

22. Butler, *Wantage Parish Diaries*, 3 February 1850.

23. Gilley, p. 128.

24. Butler, *Wantage Parish Diaries*, April 1858.

25. Stevens, *Letter Books*, 5 June 1850 and 7 October 1852.

26. Ibid., 11 May 1855.

27. Ibid., 18 June 1855.

28. Butler, *Wantage Parish Diaries*, 4 September 1864.

29. Ibid., 10–14 April 1849.

30. Anthony Russell, *The Clerical Profession* (London: SPCK, 1980), p. 106.

31. William Gresley, *The Ordinance of Confession* (1851), pp. 17–18.

32. Bennett, *Story of Bennett*, pp. 175 and 178.

33. Briscoe and Mackay, *Tractarian at Work*, pp. 57 and 118.

34. Stevens, *Letter Books*, 9 October 1866.

35. Herbert B. J. Armstrong, *A Norfolk Diary* (London: George G.

Harrap and Co., 1949), pp. 12, 66 and 118; Armstrong, *Armstrong's Norfolk Diary*, pp. 23 and 47.

36. Butler, *Wantage Parish Diaries*, 31 December 1867.

37. Frances Knight, *The Nineteenth-Century Church and English Society* (Cambridge: Cambridge University Press, 1995), p. 42.

38. Ibid., pp. 56–7.

39. Russell, p. 112 and Obelkevitch, pp. 103 and 137.

40. Obelkevitch, p. 127 and Knight, pp. 202–3.

41. Obelkevitch, pp.171–3 where he finds that the Lincolnshire clergy did not see Dissent as primarily a religious phenomenon. Also Knight, p. 202.

42. Butler, *Wantage Parish Diaries*, 28 January 1852.

43. See John Mason Neale, *The Lewes Riot: Its Causes and Consequences* (London: Masters, 1857), and J. Scobell, *The Rev. J. M. Neale and the Institution of St. Margaret's, East Grinstead* (London: Nisbett, 1857), and *A Reply to the Postcript of the Rev. John Mason Neale* (London: Nisbett, 1858).

44. Russell, p. 124.

45. John Mason Neale, *Lectures Principally on the Church Difficulties of the Present Time* (London: Cleaver, 1852), p. 234.

46. T. T. Carter, *The Doctrine of Confession in the Church of England* (London: Masters, 1869), pp. 272–3.

47. Neale, *Lectures on Church Difficulties*, pp. 235–6.

48. John Mason Neale, *The History of Pues* (1843), p. 1.

49. Newsome, *Parting of Friends*, p. 270.

50. K. S. Inglis, *Churches and the Working Classes in Victorian England* (London: RKP, 1963) p. 50.

51. F. E. Paget, *The Curate of Cumberworth* (London: Masters, 1859), pp. 19–20.

52. Butler, *Wantage Parish Diaries*, 31 December 1854.

53. Armstrong, *Armstrong's Norfolk Diary*, 12 May 1859 and 21 October 1862.

54. Briscoe and Mackay, *Tractarian at Work*, pp. 118–19.

55. Henry Newland, *Confirmation and First Communion* (1854), p. 3.

56. William Gresley, *Bernard Leslie: Second Part* (1859), pp. 163 and 166.

57. Edward Monro, *Sermons Principally on the Responsibilities of the*

Ministerial Office (London: J. H. Parker, 1850), pp. 105, 106 and 107.

58. Nigel Yates, *Anglican Ritualism in Victorian Britain 1830–1910* (Oxford: Oxford University Press, 1999), p. 107.

59. John Mason Neale, *Hierologus; or The Church Tourists* (London: James Burns, 1843), p. 72.

60. For a brief modern account, see Owen Chadwick, *The Victorian Church: Part One* (third edition, 1971), pp. 491–5.

61. Charles Le Geyt, 'Ritualism: Its Uses and Importance', in *Lectures in Defence of Church Principles Delivered by Several Clergymen at Ipswich and Norwich, 1863 and 1864* (London: Mowbray, n.d.), pp. 10 and 16.

62. Ibid., pp. 11–12.

63. Trench, *Skinner Memoir*, p. 215.

64. Armstrong, *Armstrong's Norfolk Diary*, p. 109.

65. Quoted in Yates, p. 89.

66. Ibid., p. 88.

67. See Herring, pp. 311–14, 317–19 and 341.

68. Yates, pp. 277–8.

69. Quoted in ibid., p. 96.

70. Ibid., p. 245.

71. Ibid., pp. 273–6.

Epilogue

1. See Rowell, *Vision Glorious*, p. 244.

2. Nockles, p. 326.

3. H. E. Manning, *England and Christendom* (London: Longmans, 1867) pp. lxxxiii–lxxxiv.

4. Anthony Symondson, 'Are Anglo-Catholics Catholic?', in Dwight Longenecker, *The Path to Rome: Modern Journeys to the Catholic Church* (Leominster: Gracewing, 1999), p. 226.

5. Quoted in Ker, *Newman*, pp. 720, 721.

6. Obituary in *The Daily Telegraph*, 3 August 2001.

7. See Yates, p. 370.

Further reading

A conventional bibliography would inevitably be somewhat out of proportion to the size of this book, so I have confined myself to making suggestions as to where readers can follow up some of the aspects of Tractarianism covered here, often specialist texts which themselves contain detailed bibliographies. Starting with general works on the nineteenth-century Church, the most substantial probably is that edited by G. Parsons, *Religion in Victorian Britain* (Manchester: Manchester University Press, 1988) in four volumes. Older but highly readable is Owen Chadwick's *The Victorian Church* (London: A. & C. Black, 1972) in two parts. For a longer-term perspective there is E. R. Norman, *Church and Society in England 1770–1970* (Oxford: Clarendon Press, 1976). For the Oxford Movement itself a good starting point would be Geoffrey Rowell, *The Vision Glorious: Themes and Personalities of the Catholic Revival in Anglicanism* (Oxford: Oxford University Press, 1983); there is inevitably some overlap with my present book, but there are also chapters on individuals and other aspects I have not covered. David Newsome's *The Parting of Friends: A Study of the Wilberforces and Henry Manning* (London: John Murray, 1966) is one of the finest books on the Oxford Movement, elegantly and movingly written, with a wealth of quotations from letters, and opening a window on to the whole world of nineteenth-century Anglicanism and the issues that absorbed the clergy and laity of the period. More recently, *The Oxford Movement in Context: Anglican High Churchmanship 1760–1857* (Cambridge: Cambridge University Press, 1994) by Peter Nockles is equally impressive, based on over seventeen years of research, meticulously presented, and offering a range of insights and reinterpretations on the relations between the older High Churchman and the Tractarians. Peter Toon in *Evangelical Theology 1833–1856: A Response to Tractarianism* (London: Marshall, Morgan and Scott, 1979) views Tractarianism from the perspective of the other main party in nineteenth-century Anglicanism, with some equally interesting perceptions. Alf Härdelin's *The Tractarian Understanding of the Eucharist* (Uppsala: Uppsala University Press, 1965) is another magisterial treatment of its subject, but with much on other aspects of the Oxford Movement apart from Eucharistic theology. Nigel Yates, *Anglican Ritualism in Victorian Britain 1830–1910* (Oxford: Oxford University Press, 1999) is the product of a quarter of a century of research, contains a wealth of material, much of it in the form of statistics and tables, but unfortunately for such a visual subject, no illustrations. There is little directly on the parochial aspect of Tractarianism, but there are three very useful books on various aspects of rural Christianity in the nineteenth century: Diana McClatchey, *Oxfordshire Clergy 1770–1869: A Study of the Established Church and the Role of its Clergy in Local Society* (Oxford: Clarendon Press, 1960); James Obelkevitch, *Religion and Rural Society: South Lindsey 1825–1875* (Oxford: Clarendon Press, 1976) and Frances Knight, *The Nineteenth-Century Church and English Society* (Cambridge: Cambridge University Press, 1995). For the Anglican clergy see Alan Haig, *The Victorian Clergy* (London: Croom Helm, 1984); Anthony Russell, *The Clerical Profession* (London: SPCK, 1980), and Brian Heeney, *A Different Kind of Gentleman: Parish Clergy as Professional men in Early and Mid-Victorian England* (Archon Books, 1976) both deal with the so-called 'professionalism' of the clergy in the nineteenth century, a concept I would have some reservations about if applied uncritically to the Tractarians.

As for biographies of the leading Tractarians, some have fared better than others. There are numerous studies of Newman, and various aspects of his life and thought. Meriol Trevor's two-volumed biography, *Newman: The Pillar of the Cloud* and *Newman: Light in Winter* (Basingstoke: Macmillan, 1962) are highly readable, if now rather dated, not least in the rather uncritical attitude to Newman himself. The most scholarly recent biographies are Ian Ker, *John Henry Newman: A Biography* (Oxford: Clarendon Press, 1988), and Sheridan Gilley, *Newman and his Age* (London: Darton, Longman & Todd, 1990). The former is very much centred on

Newman's ideas and some readers may find it rather 'dry' as a consequence; the latter tries to keep more of a balance between the ideas and the personality of Newman. Among the most recent specialist studies on Newman, the one by Stephen Thomas, *Newman and Heresy: The Anglican Years* (Cambridge: Cambridge University Press, 1991) stands out for its detailed and scholarly approach to the study of the evolution of Newman's theology.

John Keble has also received a steady flow of biographies in recent decades, starting with Georgina Battiscombe, *John Keble: A Study in Limitations* (London: Constable, 1963), again highly readable if marred by occasional inaccuracies. The two best modern studies are probably Brian W. Martin, *John Keble: Priest, Professor and Poet* (London: Croom Helm, 1976), and Charles R. Henery (ed.), *A Speaking Life: John Keble and the Anglican Tradition of Ministry and Art* (Leominster: Gracewing, 1995).

Richard Hurrell Froude has only attracted one modern biographer, Piers Brendon, *Hurrell Froude and the Oxford Movement* (London: Paul Elek, 1974), while Dr Pusey has attracted none. There is, however, a good collection of essays on aspects of his life and work edited by Perry Butler, *Pusey Rediscovered* (Oxford: Oxford University Press, 1983).

There are also two other good, modern collections of essays on various aspects of the Oxford Movement: Geoffrey Rowell (ed.) *Tradition Renewed: The Oxford Movement Conference Papers* (London: Darton, Longman & Todd, 1986), and Paul Vaiss (ed.) *From Oxford to the People: Reconsidering Newman and the Oxford Movement* (Leominster: Gracewing, 1996). As for collections of original documentary sources, there are again two: Eugene R. Fairweather, *The Oxford Movement* (Oxford: Oxford University Press, 1964), and Elizabeth Jay (ed.) *The Evangelical and Oxford Movements* (Cambridge: Cambridge University Press, 1983), both of which contain fewer, but more substantial extracts than this book, and the second obviously also includes writings by the Evangelicals by way of comparison.

I have obviously concentrated on the more modern studies, as many of the older works are hugely problematical in their approaches, as will have become obvious from reading this book. However, John Henry Newman's *Apologia Pro Vita Sua*, originally written in 1864, is one of the greatest spiritual autobiographies in the Christian tradition, and certainly worth reading, providing some of the reservations about it discussed in earlier chapters are kept in mind.

It is indeed difficult to know where to stop when recommending books on the Oxford Movement and nineteenth-century Anglicanism, but I hope those mentioned here will be sufficient for readers who wish to explore the subject further.

Index

141